Wide World of Words

Amsco books by Joan D. Berbrich

Fifteen Steps to Better Writing
Laugh Your Way Through Grammar
Macbeth: A Resource Book
101 Ways to Learn Vocabulary
Reading Around the World
Reading Today
Thirteen Steps to Better Writing
Wide World of Words
Writing About Amusing Things
Writing About Curious Things
Writing About Fascinating Things
Writing About People
Writing Creatively
Writing Logically
Writing Practically

JOAN D. BERBRICH, Ph.D.
Supervisor, English Department, Mineola High School, Garden City Park, New York

Wide World of Words

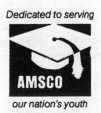

Dedicated to serving

AMSCO

our nation's youth

When ordering this book, please specify: either R 159 W or Wide World of Words

AMSCO SCHOOL PUBLICATIONS, INC.
315 Hudson Street   New York, N.Y. 10013

Acknowledgments

Grateful acknowledgment is made to the following sources for permission to use copyrighted materials, which appear in this book on the pages indicated.

King Features. Page 75. "Boner's Ark" strip by Addison. © King Features Syndicate, 1972.

Los Angeles Times. Page 77. "Figments" strip by Dale Hale. © Los Angeles Times, 1972. Reprinted with permission.

New York Teacher. Page 76. "Croker" strip by Brian Pickering. © *New York Teacher,* 1972.

Vital Speeches of the Day. Page 8. Quotation from "Crime in Industry" by Harvey S. Gellman. © *Vital Speeches of the Day,* 1970.

ISBN 0-87720-340-7

To the Student

The world you live in is a world of words.

You don't believe it? Imagine that you're introducing a Martian to American civilization. Describe for him a simple game of baseball. You'll have trouble getting to first base, much less to home plate! Obviously, there are dozens of words he must understand before he will know what a line drive is, or a home run.

Try explaining to the same Martian what an automobile is . . . or a television set . . . or a school. A school, you say, is "a large building in which students learn and teachers teach." But what is a "building"? What are "students"? "Teachers"? What does "large" mean? What is it "to learn" or "to teach"? You see the problem?

To describe the simplest object, many words are needed. But by now, you already have a huge vocabulary. You know what a "school" is, what a "building" is, what "learning" means. Why, then, learn more?

Think about it a moment and you'll know the answer. When you were two years old, your world was small and you needed only a few words: words like *milk*, *ball*, *hurt*, *gimme*. By the time you were five, your world had grown larger and you needed more words: words like *friend*, *swings*, *candy*, *circus*. Since then your world has expanded still more, and you have acquired sophisticated words like *democracy*, *literature*, and *metropolis* and technical words like *transistor*, *carburetor*, and *stereophonic*.

But your world has not stopped growing. It is growing now, and it will continue to grow. And your ability to handle that world will depend in part on whether your knowledge of words has grown, too.

Consider the mass media for a moment. Do you know what *electronic amplification* is? Or *feedback*? Or *synchronization*?

Consider sports. Do you know what *coordination* is? Or *agility*? Would you recognize a *palomino*? What would you do with a *stirrup*?

Consider the future . . . *your* future. What is a *transplant*? How would *cloning* affect life? Would you like to own (or be) a *cyborg*?

It is a little frightening to realize the tremendous number of words you must master. The caveman may have gotten by with an occasional "ugh," and even your grandfather needed far fewer words than you do. Technological progress has not only made the world wider, but it has made wider too the world of words.

Learning new words need not be frightening, though. The trick is to learn words in groups. That's the way you learned the first words you used. It's still the easiest way. If, for example, you spent three hours with a mechanic taking a car apart and putting it together again, you would learn a dozen new words in a very short time. If you sat in on rehearsals of a play, even one rehearsal, your dramatic vocabulary would increase dramatically! And the fastest way to teach that Martian what a baseball game is would be to give him a bat and ball and show him how to play.

If we had more money and more time, this direct experience would be the most painless—and easiest—way to learn new words. Unfortunately, it's not usually possible to take you on a trip to Europe so that you can learn what a *visa* is and how it differs from a *passport*. And it's certainly not feasible to shoot you to the moon so that you can observe, firsthand, the operation of a *moon crawler*. So you turn to the second-best—to vicarious experience.

Take a trip vicariously (Part Seven). Decide whether to travel by Amtrak or by jet. Worry about *vehicular homicide* and *hairpin turns*. Wonder how your stomach will react to *cruising* at 600 mph or to *inverted flying*. In no time you will have mastered many new words dealing with moving vehicles and with traveling.

This method will help you to learn related words, too. *Flailing arms* and *flamboyant poses* will become part of your permanent vocabulary if you connect them to the Roller Derby; *maximum* and *minimum* become unforgettably important when you're driving and there's a police car behind you; and once you've ridden a motorcycle (even vicariously), you'll remember what *rugged terrain* is and the result of reaching the *vibration point* at 6,000 r.p.m.

It will help, too, if you become a *word-watcher*. Watch for these and other new words when you read a newspaper or listen to television. Find them in the conversation of friends, and notice the way some of them jump from field to field (e.g., *contour*—from farming to car seats).

Take your Martian friend along, and through his fresh, eager eyes, wander through the Wide World of Words. It should be an exciting and fruitful journey for both of you!

Contents

One. The Word Detective at Work

1. A Detection Kit   *1*
2. Two Kinds of Fingerprints   *4*
3. Moulages and Trouser Cuffs   *7*
4. The Art of Deduction   *11*
5. Detecting With a Dictionary   *14*
6. Police Patrol   *17*
7. Rogues' Gallery   *20*
8. Mini-Mysteries   *24*

Two. Word Families—and Friends

1. What's in a Name?   *26*
2. Self: Outer View   *30*
3. Self: Inner View   *34*
4. Clothes Make the Man (or Woman)!   *36*
5. Eat to Live? Or Live to Eat?   *41*
6. A House Is Not a Home . . .   *44*
7. School Bells Ring   *48*
8. Seven-League Boots   *52*
9. Midget Mysteries   *55*

Three. Words to Tickle the Funny Bone

1. Laugh-in   *57*
2. Riddles and Puns   *60*
3. Pedantry Prevails   *64*
4. Pop Poetry   *66*
5. Catastrophe With a Banana Peel   *69*
6. Sights and Sounds   *72*
7. Comic-Strip Mysteries   *75*

Four. The Mass Media, in So Many Words

1. Media Mania   *78*
2. The Boob Tube   *81*
3. The Celluloid Myth   *83*
4. Stop the Press!   *86*
5. Air Waves   *88*
6. Say Cheese!   *91*
7. It's Free!   *94*
8. Political Arena   *97*
9. Media Mysteries   *100*

Five. Putting in a Good Word for Animals

1. Big-Game Hunting   *102*
2. The Zoo Story   *106*
3. With Rod and Reel   *109*
4. First Flight   *112*
5. The Insect World   *116*
6. Larking With Livestock   *119*
7. Peripatetic Pets   *123*
8. Mammalian (and Nonmammalian) Mysteries   *127*

Six. The Last Word About Sports

1. Ball Barrage   *130*
2. Racquet Squad   *134*
3. To the Swift   *137*
4. In the Saddle   *141*
5. Snow Magic   *145*
6. On Target!   *148*
7. In the Depths   *151*
8. Mystery Morsels   *154*

Seven. Words to Travel By

1. A Concrete Nation *156*
2. On a Bicycle Built For . . . *160*
3. The Roller Derby *163*
4. The Lonely Whistle *166*
5. The Wild Blue Yonder *169*
6. Mongrel Mysteries *172*

Eight. Words for Tomorrow

1. A Medley of Monsters *174*
2. Earth to Mars *177*
3. Life in the Year 2000 *181*
4. The Age of Superman *184*
5. Puzzles for Posterity *187*

Nine. A Word for Everything

1. Animal Crackers *188*
2. Color Me Green! *191*
3. On Your Mettle! *194*
4. Jinks With Jewelry *196*
5. Flaunting Flowers *200*
6. Vocations and Avocations *203*
7. Worked-over Words *205*
8. Body-Building *208*

Ten. You're Twisting My Words

1. Be a Name-Dropper *210*
2. Forward-Reverse *213*
3. Cracking the Code *215*
4. Which Is the Kate That . . . ? *217*
5. Words Within Words *220*
6. Bittersweet *222*
7. Patterns to Ponder *227*
8. Happiness Is . . . a Warm Puppy *230*
9. Spoke Screen *233*

Eleven. Wordplay

1. Casual Crosswords *237*
2. Add-a-Letter *241*
3. Change-about *243*
4. Pyramid Play *245*
5. From One, Many! *248*
6. Acrostic Crossfire *250*
7. Circle Circus *253*
8. Monogram Mania *258*
9. Harebrained Homonyms *260*

Topical Reference Guide *263*

Index *263*

One. The Word Detective at Work

1

A Detection Kit

Every workman needs good tools. The carpenter, the auto mechanic, the jeweler—all need special equipment. So does the modern detective. A hundred years ago, Sherlock Holmes, the greatest of all fictional detectives, could manage with a magnifying glass and his brain—but times have changed. The criminal is smarter, and the detective must be, too. So here's Lesson #1—on how to be a detective!

"Captain Sanders speaking. Homicide."

Sanders listened intently to the choked, terrified voice of the witness, jotted down an address, then turned to a couple of detectives across the room. "Another murder—this one on East Third!" he said sharply. "Let's go!"

A few minutes later, at the entrance to a cul-de-sac (blind alley), the police car screeched to a stop. The victim was a middle-aged male who had been robbed and shot. But who was he? His wallet was missing. He had no letters, no cards of identification.

The police could check the Missing Persons Bureau, of course, but what else could they do? Below are pictures of three possible methods of identification available to Captain Sanders. Can you identify each of them?

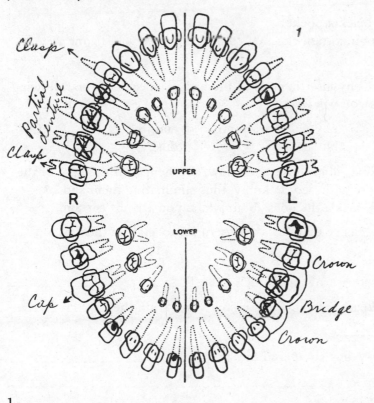

2. _

1. _

3. _

The first, of course, is a dental chart showing fillings, extractions, a cap, a bridge, and a plate. Police can circulate copies of the dental chart to all the dentists in the area to see if any one of them can identify the person whose chart it is.

The second is a fingerprint, complete with arches, loops, and whorls. If the victim's prints are already on file with the local police or with the F.B.I. in Washington, this method of identification is fast and sure.

The third is a photograph that can be printed in newspapers and distributed to police stations throughout the country. Sometimes a description of a visible birthmark will accompany the picture.

Any one of these methods can result in a positive identification. But identifying the victim is only one-half the work of the police. They must also identify the criminal—and this is considerably more difficult. Few criminals cooperate by staying quietly at the scene of the crime. Occasionally one leaves fingerprints (although most now wear gloves), but none leaves a photograph or a dental chart!

Fortunately, almost all of them do leave one or two clues, and, once they are considered suspects, they often involuntarily provide a few more. Through these clues, the police can often eliminate some suspects and eventually arrive at a conclusive identification.

Within 24 hours, Captain Sanders and his men had taken a suspect into custody. These were their clues:

At the scene: a footprint
a bullet
a physical description of the criminal, given by a witness
On the suspect: a bloodstain
a gun
some dust from a jacket pocket
A block away: the victim's wallet in a trash can. (Of course, the money was gone.)

I. Complete the following statements by inserting one of these clues in each of the following blanks. These are the expressions you will write:

footprint   physical description   gun
bullet   bloodstain   dust

Use a detective's technique: (1) first fill in those you know; (2) then, with the help of the process of elimination (i.e., first doing those you know, thus eliminating them and narrowing the remaining choices), tackle the ones about which you are not certain.

1. The police used *serology*, the science that deals with serums, to analyze the _____

_____ .

2. They made a *moulage*, a plaster cast, of the _____.

3. They used an identikit to make a model of the criminal's face from the _____

_____ .

4. With a *comparison microscope*, they compared the _____

to one they shot from the suspect's _____
and found the two had similar markings.

5. With a vacuum they collected _____ and,

after analyzing it, were able to prove that the suspect had had the victim's wallet in his possession.

Victim identified.
Criminal identified.
Case closed.

*   *   *

A good detective cultivates two "tools" of his trade—memory and deduction. Test *your* ability to *remember* and *deduce*.

II. To Test Your Memory

Answers to the following questions were given in the text. Can you remember them?

1. What is a *moulage*? _____

2. What is *serology*? _____

3. What is the function of a *comparison microscope*? _____

_____

4. What is a *cul-de-sac*? _____

5. What is meant by the *process of elimination*? _____

_____

_____

III. To Test Your Deductive Powers

Answers to the following questions were *not* given directly in the text, but you should be able to *deduce* the answers.

1. What does *homicide* mean? _____

_____

2. What is a *clue*? _____

_____

3. "Sanders listened *intently* to the choked, terrified voice of the witness." Did he listen *carefully* or *impatiently*? _____

4. What is meant by a *conclusive* identification? _____

_____

5. What does the verb *deduce* mean? What is meant by *deductive* powers? What does *deduction* mean?

   (*a*) deduce   _____

   (*b*) deductive   _____

   (*c*) deduction   _____

2
Two Kinds of Fingerprints

Fingerprints are distinctive. No one else in the world has fingerprints exactly like yours. Look closely at the tips of your fingers. Notice the arches and loops and whorls? That particular pattern was formed before you were born; it will continue, unchanged, for as long as you live. You cannot alter your fingerprints, and no one else (without extraordinary measures like skin grafting) can alter them for you.

Fingerprints are so much a part of you that they can establish your identification at any time during your life. For this reason, detectives depend on them frequently.

Words are not human and therefore have no fingerprints—but they do have distinctive characteristics that help to identify and define them. Let's look for some word "fingerprints."

1. *Question:* Can you find a distinctive characteristic that is common to all five of the following words?

> magnify   magnanimous   magnitude
> magnificent   magnate

Answer: They all begin with the word element *magni* or *magna*, meaning "great," or "large," or "big." (Knowing that, you are halfway to knowing the meaning of all five words.)

2. *Question:* Can you find a distinctive characteristic that is common to these five words?

> microscope   microphone   microscopic
> microbe   microfilm

Answer: They all begin with the word element *micro*, meaning "very small."

Remember that fingerprints, like all clues, are worthless until you interpret them correctly and use them. Read again the five *magni* words and the five *micro* words. Then check these additional clues.

> a. *Phono* (sound or voice) and *film* are words with which you are already familiar.
> b. *Scope* (see) is almost as familiar. It is a root, that is, the main part of a word. You know it in tele*scope* and peri*scope*.
> c. *Animus* (or *anima*), another root, means "mind" or "soul."

I. Now, keeping all of these clues in mind, see if you can complete the following paragraphs by placing the five *magni* words and the five *micro* words in the correct blanks. Use each word only once. (Remember the process of elimination!)

The (1) _____ (*big man in business*) was a millionaire, but he

was still furious when a thief stole his $100 watch, a (2) _____

(*splendid, superb*) timepiece made in Switzerland. When he spotted a policeman at the end

of the street, he used a (3) _____ (*an instrument that converts

small sounds into big ones*) that had been installed in his car to summon him.

"That—that human (4) _____ (*minute life form; germ*) who

just ran down the street stole my watch," he said bitterly. "It is a crime of such (5) _____

_____ (*large size*) that no punishment can be too harsh!"

The thief had left behind a single hair. The police placed this under a (6) _____

_____ (*an instrument that permits you to see something extremely small*) that they took from the trunk of their car. "Ah, ha!" said the Inspector. "I see that the thief is a 70-year-old male, he is French, and he is anemic!"

"That's interesting," said the millionaire. "Here's something else you should know. He

has (7)_____ (*very small; so small you can hardly see them*) eyes. In fact, his eyes are so small I never did find out what color they are."

"Never mind," said the Inspector. "We will study our photos of thieves on our (8)____

_____ (*a film on which items are greatly reduced in size*) reader. We shall be back in an hour."

One hour later the Inspector returned with an old man. "Here is the thief," he announced proudly. "He was planning to sell your watch in order to buy milk for his starving grandchild."

The millionaire scowled. "I do not wish to (9)_____ (*make larger*) his guilt," he said, "but he is a danger to society. He should be punished by the law." Then a smile appeared on his face. "But first," he added, as he handed the old man five thin dimes, "first let him buy that bottle of milk for his starving grandchild! I do,

after all, have a reputation for being (10)_____ (*noble-minded; generous in granting forgiveness*).

II. To Test Your Memory

1. What does *magnitude* mean? _____

2. What is a *microbe*? _____

3. What instrument could you use that would permit you to speak softly and still be heard

   throughout a large auditorium? _____

4. What instrument might you use in the library if you wish to review all the issues of the *New York Times* published during the month of September, 1953? (The pages are

   photographed, on a greatly reduced scale, and then projected.)_____

   _____

5. What is the *root* of a word? _____

   _____

   _____

III. To Test Your Deductive Powers

1. Would the word *magnate* generally refer to an industrial leader or a very tall man?

   _____

2. Does *distinctive* mean (*a*) unusual; clearly different *or* (*b*) attractive? ____

3. Name two kinds of information about a human being that can sometimes be discovered by analyzing a single hair from his head. _____

   _____

4. "You cannot alter your fingerprints." What does *alter* mean? _____

5. If *anima* means "mind" or "soul" or "life," and *in* means "not" or "without," why would a table properly be called an *inanimate* object? _____

   _____

3
Moulages and Trouser Cuffs

For the amateur detective, some of the most fascinating clues are not the fingerprints of the victim (primary clues) but those that *surround* the crime (secondary clues). That large footprint outside the window, this bit of fluff in a trouser cuff, the tarnished coat button that rolled into the corner, or the dab of clayish mud left on the rug—these clues, properly analyzed and interpreted, tell their own vivid story.

A moulage of the footprint may reveal that the criminal is over six feet tall, weighs about 180 pounds, and walks with his toes turned in. The bit of fluff in the trouser cuff may have asbestos in it and lead to the factory in which he works. The stray button may be recognized by a particular tailor or may bear the insignia of a club of which he is a member. And that clayish mud may be found in only one nearby tract of land—the one behind his house where, in peaceable moments, he tenderly cultivates hybrid roses.

A word, too, can be identified by secondary clues—by the words that precede it or the words that follow it, by the general tone of a paragraph, by a whole series of details that illustrate it.

Suppose you came across this sentence:

"At the trial Jackson was calm and optimistic as he asserted his innocence."

Suppose further that you did not know the meaning of *asserted* and that no dictionary was available. What could you do?

First, of course, you look at the word itself—but *asserted* doesn't contain many clues. Its placement in the sentence and the "ed" ending tell you that it is a verb in the past tense, but that helps only a little.

Next you turn to secondary clues. Whatever was happening was happening at a trial, and Jackson's innocence had been called into question. Since he was optimistic and calm, he was probably not denying his innocence but defending it . . . stating it forcefully. And that is exactly what *asserted* means.

I. In each of the following sentences (taken from newspapers and other periodicals) there is at least one clue that will help you to define the italicized word. Try to figure out a definition for each. Then, in the space provided, write the definition and explain briefly how the rest of the sentence helped you to arrive at a solution.

1. "One of the boats was fire-bombed. Since it was in a wooden boathouse, the only thing we *salvaged* was an anchor." (*Newsday*, April 3, 1972)

   DEFINITION: _____

   EXPLANATION: _____

   _____

   _____

2. "He could find no real *motive* for suicide—the engineer had money in the bank, had a good job and was a confirmed family man." (*New York Times*, March 12, 1972)

   DEFINITION: _____

   EXPLANATION: _____

   _____

   _____

3. "Burglary is defined as the breaking into of a home or store followed by a theft without a *confrontation* with an occupant. . . . Robbery is theft from a person by force or threat of force, in a holdup or a mugging." (*New York Times*, December 20, 1970)

   DEFINITION: _____

   EXPLANATION: _____

   _____

   _____

4. "The marine thief is not *deterred* by motor locks or chained boats." (*Newsday*, September 23, 1970)

   DEFINITION: _____

   EXPLANATION: _____

   _____

   _____

5. "Six hours later they had *amassed* enough evidence to know what type of car they were looking for." (*Newsday*, November 7, 1970)

   DEFINITION: _____

   EXPLANATION: _____

   _____

   _____

6. "Every passenger is subject to a mini-*interrogation* in which the inspector gathers such basic intelligence as where the passenger has been travelling and for how long." (*New York Times*, November 29, 1970)

   DEFINITION: _____

   EXPLANATION: _____

   _____

   _____

7. "I am not a gambler, yet I am willing to bet any computer user that his computer installation is *vulnerable* to theft and abuse. . . . There are plenty of examples to show that most computer installations today have inadequate controls to protect them against theft or damage to programs or data." ("Crime in Industry" by Harvey S. Gellman in *Vital Speeches of the Day*, December 15, 1970)

   DEFINITION: _____

   EXPLANATION: _____

   _____

   _____

8. "In neighborhoods where the policeman was once a figure of majestic authority, he now often confronts jeering *hostility*." ("What Is Law and Order?" editorial in *The Saturday Evening Post*, October 19, 1968)

DEFINITION: _____

EXPLANATION: _____

_____

_____

9. "Various studies consistently show that an overwhelming majority of the adult population believe our courts do not deal *rigorously* enough with criminals. But other studies show that this attitude tends to break down, in favor of dealing gently, when a specific defendant is under consideration." (*National Review*, April 22, 1969)

DEFINITION: _____

EXPLANATION: _____

_____

_____

10. "After half an hour in a grounded plane with no air conditioning, the *irate* captain finally convinced the airport controllers that there was no skyjacker." (*Time*, October 9, 1972)

DEFINITION: _____

EXPLANATION: _____

_____

_____

II. Now that you have made the clues work for you, reverse the process and see if you can place the same 10 words into appropriate blanks in the sentences that follow them.

amassed	interrogation	rigorously
confrontation	irate	salvaged
deterred	motive	vulnerable
hostility		

1. The _____ of the witness was not surprising, since he was the brother of the defendant.

2. In order to obtain the information he needed, the district attorney conducted an intense _____ of the witness.

3. When they discovered that the thief was heavily in debt, they were sure they knew his _____ for committing the crime.

4. When a group of hoodlums meets a group of policemen, an unpleasant _____ is almost inevitable.

5. Within 10 years he _____ enough money to retire.

6. "The four students who didn't do their homework will report for detention for three days," said the _____ teacher.

7. Unfortunately, the academic delinquent is seldom _____ from future misconduct even by three days of detention.

8. After the flood, only a brass lamp and a marble statue were _____.

9. "I will deal _____ even with petty thieves," said the crime commissioner as he began his new term of office.

10. The sensitive person is _____ to insults as the wealthy person is _____ to threats. (same word in both blanks)

4
The Art of Deduction

Deduction *is* an art. It is the art by which you take information you already have, think about it, and arrive at a new idea or conclusion. It is a very useful art, since it exercises your mental muscles and broadens your knowledge.

I. Below are 10 case studies. Each has two parts: the first is a mini-biography of a person, and the second is the definition of a word that was named after that person. Work with each case study. Read both parts and try to figure out either the name of the person or the word that is the namesake. If you succeed in finding one of the two, you should be able to *deduce* the other from it.

Example:

A

This English earl was a gambler who disliked having to stop playing in order to eat. He supposedly was given to eating informally at the gaming table. His namesake was developed *for* him.

The man: _

B

This namesake is a favorite lunchtime food. It is made of two slices of bread with meat or some other filling between the slices.

The namesake: _

Solution:

In this particular case study it is easy to identify the namesake—the word *sandwich*. With this information plus Part A, you may be able to deduce that the person involved is the Earl of Sandwich (specifically John Montagu, the Fourth Earl of Sandwich, 1718–1792). In some of the case studies, however, it will be easier to identify the person and from that deduce the namesake.

Now try *your* deductive powers on the 10 case studies that follow. (An alphabetical list of the subjects of the 10 case studies appears at the end of the exercise. Refer to them *only* if you must!)

A

1. This man was a famous French general and emperor of France in the 19th century. Although he won many battles, he is remembered for a battle he lost: Waterloo.

   The man: _

2. This Scottish engineer experimented with road making in the early 19th century. The road that he finally invented was so much better than the old dirt roads that it revolutionized transportation in the United States and England.

B

This namesake is a rectangular piece of pastry covered with icing and filled with custard cream.

The namesake: _

This namesake is a roadbed made of small stones crushed together, then bound either with stone dust and water or with tar.

The man: _

The namesake: _

3. This Englishman, a land agent in Ireland in the 1880's, was so cruel in evicting tenants that his employees refused to cooperate with him.

   This namesake is a protest demonstrated by a refusal to buy a particular product or to deal with a particular firm.

   The man: _

   The namesake: _

4. This French soldier admired Napoleon excessively. He was devoted to him and was unable to see the emperor's faults.

   This namesake is a fanatical, unthinking patriotism for one's country or, more recently, excessive loyalty to one's sex.

   The man: _

   The namesake: _

5. This French economist made such sharp cuts in the budget that people had to make great sacrifices and felt they had been reduced to shadows.

   This namesake is a profile portrait or outline of an object sketched usually in black or cut out of black paper and pasted against a lighter background.

   The man: _

   The namesake: _

6. This French woman practically ruled France during the reign of Louis XV. In addition, she had a reputation as a beauty and a leader of fashion.

   This namesake is a hair style, used by men and women, in which the hair is swept up high over the forehead.

   The woman: _ _ _ _ _ _ _ _ _ _ _ _ _ _ _ _ _ _

   The namesake: _

7. This German physician worked first with animal magnetism and then claimed to be able to effect magnetic cures through hypnotism.

   This namesake is a kind of individual or group hypnotism that enthralls the subject, sometimes making him insensible to pain and unable to think clearly.

   The man: _ _ _ _ _ _ _ _ _ _ _ _ _ _ _ _ _ _

   The namesake: _

8. This Texan cattleman didn't bother to brand his cattle. As a result many of them, especially calves, were picked up by other ranchers.

   This namesake is an unbranded calf (one that doesn't belong to anybody). Today it also refers to a human being who goes his own way, refusing to belong to conventional groups.

   The man: _ _ _ _ _ _ _ _ _ _ _ _ _ _ _ _ _ _

   The namesake: _

9. This American woman dedicated her life to woman's rights. In an attempt to help women free themselves from clumsy and uncomfortable clothing, she recommended that they wear loose trousers under a short skirt.

   This namesake is an outfit for women. It is loose trousers, sometimes gathered at the ankles. Today it sometimes refers to loose pants gathered above the knee and worn for athletic events.

   The woman: _ _ _ _ _ _ _ _ _ _ _ _ _ _ _ _ _ _

   The namesake: _

10. This man was elected governor of Massachusetts in 1810. In his second term, he and his supporters rearranged the boundaries of an election district so that their party would retain control.

The man: _____

This namesake is a political maneuver that arranges the boundaries of election districts for the advantage of one party. The new shapes of the election districts often resemble an octopus or some other monstrous creature.

The namesake: _____

Subjects of the 10 case studies:

Amelia Bloomer (1818–1894)
Charles C. Boycott (1832–1897)
Nicholas Chauvin (19th century)
Elbridge Gerry (1744–1814)
Samuel Maverick (1803–1870)
John L. McAdam (1756–1836)
Franz Mesmer (1734–1815)
Napoleon I (1769–1821)
Marquise de Pompadour (1721–1764)
Étienne de Silhouette (1709–1767)

II. To Test Your Memory

1. A road made of crushed stones is known as a _____ road.

2. A profile portrait sketched in black is called a _____.

3. A person who goes his own way regardless of the opinions of others is sometimes

   known as a _____.

4. A political maneuver that unfairly reshapes an election district is called _____

   _____.

5. An economic protest during which people refuse to buy a particular product is a _____

   _____.

III. To Test Your Deductive Powers

1. *Mini* as a prefix (as in *mini-biography*) means _____.

2. What does *namesake* mean? _____

   _____

3. A collection of meaningful data about an individual is called a _____.

4. Is the devotion of a *fanatical* person generally based on reason? _____

5. Is *gerrymandering* a democratic process? Explain briefly. _____

   _____

   _____

5
Detecting With a Dictionary

A detective must be accurate: he must be absolutely certain that he interprets correctly all that he hears or reads.

A detective must be fast: slowness may hinder both his safety and his success.

A detective must be sensitive: he must be aware of the nuances (slight variations) in the speech and feelings of others.

Much of the knowledge a detective needs can be found in any dictionary—even a pocket dictionary. Your dictionary is a tool you should use daily. Here are a few practice bouts that will sharpen your skill; they may even make you a dedicated dictionary detective!

I. In the Old West, about a hundred years ago, a sheriff captured a robber. Here is a bit of their conversation. Use a dictionary to define the italicized words so that you know exactly what occurred.

"I'll confess!" the *desperado* shouted to the sheriff. "I'm the one who held up the stagecoach. I *disguised* myself as a beautiful young girl so that no one would recognize me!"

"If you hope for *leniency*," said the sheriff, "you will tell us where the *booty* is."

There was a pause. Then the desperado said *sullenly*, "In a *cache* in the cliff just behind the jail."

The sheriff smiled. "Very *appropriate*," he said as he locked the cell door and threw away the key.

1. desperado _____

2. disguised _____

3. leniency _____

4. booty _____

5. sullenly _____

6. cache _____

7. appropriate _____

II. A detective must work quickly as well as accurately. Using a dictionary, in five minutes find words beginning with the prefix *sub*, meaning "under," that fit the following definitions:

1. to conquer or to bring under control

1. sub _____

2. to rent an apartment (one that *you* rent) to someone else

2. sub _____

3. to place under water or any other liquid

3. sub _____

4. to yield to the will of another or to offer something to the consideration of another

4. sub _____

5. to sign one's name to; to agree

5. sub _____

III. A detective must also be able to distinguish between two related words. With the help of the dictionary, write definitions after the two words in each of the following pairs. Then prove you have detected the difference between the two words by answering the related questions.

1. subsidy _

   bonus _

   Related question: Would you hope to receive a *subsidy* or a *bonus* if you did

   more work than your contract called for? _ _ _ _ _ _ _ _ _ _ _ _ _ _ _ _

2. plaintiff _

   defendant _

   Related question: Would you rather be a *plaintiff* or a *defendant*? Explain.

   _

   _

3. embezzlement _

   theft _

   Related question: Would *embezzlement* or *theft* more exactly describe the crime of a bank president who took money from the accounts of the bank's

   depositors? _ _ _ _ _ _ _ _ _ _ _ _ _ _ _ _ _ _ _

IV. A detective must also be sensitive to the nuances (slight variations) in the meanings of words. With the help of a dictionary, try to answer the following questions:

1. Would you use *assassination* or *execution* to describe the murder of a United States

   Senator? _

2. Would a person who has an irresistible impulse to set fires be properly called an *arsonist*

   or a *pyromaniac*? _ _ _ _ _ _ _ _ _ _ _ _ _ _ _ _

3. If a burglar alarm sounded from two o'clock until half past two without stopping,

   would you say it sounded *continually* or *continuously*? _ _ _ _ _ _ _ _ _ _ _ _ _ _ _ _ _ _

4. If you betray your best friend, are you guilty of *treachery* or *treason*? _ _ _ _ _ _ _ _ _ _

5. Is it *unjust* or *illegal* to go through a red light? _ _ _ _ _ _ _ _ _ _ _ _ _

V. Here are a few more things every detective should know. What is the difference between

1. a *sentence* and a *verdict*? _

   _

   _

2. a *misdemeanor* and a *felony*? _

3. a *burglary* and a *robbery*? --

----

4. *manslaughter* and *murder*? ---

----

5. an *acquittal* and a *pardon*? --

6
Police Patrol

Occupation: member of the police force
Duties: to return a lost two-year-old to his mother; to apprehend (take into custody) an armed killer; to stop impatient drivers from demolishing each other's cars; to write reports
Payment: jeers and cheers, bullets and bouquets

"A policeman's lot is not a happy one," sang Gilbert and Sullivan about 100 years ago. Happy or not, the policeman's life is varied and challenging, and the words related to police work are varied and challenging, too.

I. Who?

A. In London, Sir Robert Peel started England's first organized police force in 1829. These early policemen wore blue swallow-tailed coats, high collars, and black top hats. They were nicknamed (1) _ _ _ _ _ _ _ _ _ _ _ _ _ _ _ after Sir *Robert*.

In New York, George Washington Matsell was appointed the first chief of police in 1845. The men who worked under him wore eight-pointed *copper* badges. From this means of identification came the nickname (2) _ _ _ _ _ _ _ _ _ _ _ _ and its shortened form _ _ _ _ _ _ .

In Tennessee, in 1933, "Machine Gun" Kelly stared with terror at the *government men* (F.B.I. agents) who were pursuing him. "Don't shoot, (3) _ _ _ _ _ _ _ _ _ _ _ _ !" he begged, thus starting another famous nickname.

B. Here are a few more people who work in or with the police department. See if you can match the titles in the first column with the descriptions of their jobs in the second column.

_ _ _ _ 1. medical examiner   *a.* deciphers secret codes

_ _ _ _ 2. coroner   *b.* ascertains cause of death of those who die by violence

_ _ _ _ 3. cryptographer   *c.* delivers summonses ordering people to appear in court

_ _ _ _ 4. serologist   *d.* investigates by inquest any death occurring under suspicious circumstances

_ _ _ _ 5. process server

   e. identifies and classifies blood and saliva stains

II. What?

The police are concerned with all sorts of things:

A. *Criminals*, for instance. Can you match the criminal with his description?

arsonist	hijacker	murderer
burglar	kidnapper	skyjacker
embezzler	robber	smuggler
forger	perjurer	

1. This fellow lies under oath. _____

2. This fellow kills. _____

3. This fellow starts fires in order to collect insurance or to conceal evidence of another crime. _____

4. This fellow breaks into houses to steal goods. _____

5. This fellow steals goods from trucks, trains, etc. _____

6. This fellow takes someone by force and holds him for ransom. _____

7. This fellow copies the signatures of others. _____

8. This fellow steals from people, often using violence. _____

9. This fellow brings goods into a country unlawfully. _____

10. This fellow takes over airplanes, often for ransom. _____

11. This fellow steals money that has been entrusted to him. _____

B. And with *evidence*. Can you match the following relevant (related) terms to their definitions?

____ 1. hearsay evidence

____ 2. allegation

____ 3. dying declaration

____ 4. cross examination

____ 5. privileged communication

____ 6. circumstantial evidence

____ 7. testimony

____ 8. affidavit

____ 9. subpoena

____ 10. statute

a. statement offered without proof

b. statement made to a lawyer or doctor that the listener cannot be forced to repeat

c. statement made just before death; usually accepted as true

d. an established law of a government

e. statement made in court by a witness sworn to tell the truth

f. legal writ requiring someone's appearance in court

g. evidence based on what someone has heard from others

h. close questioning of a witness by the opposing side

i. evidence that does not directly prove a defendant guilty but that does strongly suggest his guilt

j. written declaration made under oath

III. Where?

This time try to match the places in the first column with their descriptions in the second column.

____ 1. precinct

____ 2. beat

____ 3. premises

____ 4. jurisdiction

____ 5. venue

a. the area regularly covered by a particular policeman

b. the area (either geographical or judicial) in which one has the power to apply the law

c. a police station in a particular section of a city

d. location where a crime is committed and in which the trial would be held

e. a building or part of a building

7
Rogues' Gallery

Call them mug shots—or a rogues' gallery—or just plain pictures. The collection of photographs that every police department throughout the nation maintains is one of its most valuable assets. The victim who has caught a glimpse of his assailant can thumb rapidly through the photographs and can often make a fast and sure identification.

There's one problem, though: many people do not know how to *see*. It's easy to make a mistake unless you have trained your eyes to observe and your mind to record.

Here's one picture to serve as a test case (identity withheld until later). Look at it closely.

Now let's try to list some of the salient (striking; conspicuous) features:

1

  a. long, full sideburns and beard, graying
  b. hair slightly wavy, receding at part, which is on the left side
  c. eyebrows thick, almost joining at the bridge of the nose
  d. high, broad forehead
  e. eyes dark and narrow with low, heavy lids
  f. general shape of head: rectangular
  g. nose large, slightly pendulous (hanging) with arched bridge
  h. ears close to head
  i. wrinkles below eyes and below cheeks
  j. upper lip thin; lower lip full and slightly protruding

I. Does he *look* like a criminal? _ _ _ _ _ _ If your answer is yes, what kind of criminal?

_ If your answer is no, what does he look like? _ _ _ _ _ _ _ _ _ _ _ _

_ _ _ _ _ _ _ _ _ _ _ _ (identity still withheld until later)

II. Here's your own private rogues' gallery on which to practice. Study each picture closely. Then write below each picture a description of five salient characteristics. Finish by guessing what kind of person each was.

2

3

a. --------------------------------

b. --------------------------------

c. --------------------------------

d. --------------------------------

e. --------------------------------

What kind of person was he?

----

a. --------------------------------

b. --------------------------------

c. --------------------------------

d. --------------------------------

e. --------------------------------

What kind of person was she?

4

5

a. --------------------------------

b. --------------------------------

c. --------------------------------

d. --------------------------------

e. --------------------------------

What kind of person was she?

----

a. --------------------------------

b. --------------------------------

c. --------------------------------

d. --------------------------------

e. --------------------------------

What kind of person was he?

6

7

a. _____

b. _____

c. _____

d. _____

e. _____

What kind of person was he?

_____

a. _____

b. _____

c. _____

d. _____

e. _____

What kind of person was she?

_____

Before you go on to the next part of this chapter, you may find it interesting to compare notes with other students.

III. Now that you have described and tried to identify the seven people whose pictures appear on the preceding pages, let's zoom in on positive identifications. This time you are given two additional types of clues: a mini-biography and the correct name scrambled. Read the mini-biography first. Then make another guess. Finally, unscramble the name, and you will arrive at positive identification!

1. This man became president, prophet, and high priest of the Mormon Church in 1844. A few years later he led the Mormons to Utah, where they founded Salt Lake City. He had 12 wives.

    Name scrambled: GHAMRIB GOUNY   Actual name: _____

2. This man was born in Maryland and became an actor. After the Civil War, he was despondent over the defeat of the South. On April 14, 1865, he assassinated President Abraham Lincoln.

    Name scrambled: NHOJ KEWILS THOBO

        Actual name: _____

3. This woman was active in the antislavery movement during the Civil War. Later she worked for woman suffrage and for prison reform. She wrote "The Battle Hymn of the Republic."

   Name scrambled: AUJIL DRAW WOEH

   Actual name: _____

4. This woman nursed wounded soldiers in the Civil War and again in the Franco-Prussian War. In 1881 she founded and became the first president of the American Red Cross.

   Name scrambled: LARAC TRABON   Actual name: _____

5. This man was a famous hunter and explorer. After being captured by Indians, he was adopted by them as a member of the tribe but later escaped. A city on the Kentucky River has been named after him.

   Name scrambled: LAINED ONOBE   Actual name: _____

6. This man was a lawyer and a poet. During the War of 1812, he was held for a brief time on a British ship while the British bombarded Fort McHenry. At dawn, on September 14, 1814, the American flag was still flying over the fort. As a result of this experience, he wrote "The Star-Spangled Banner."

   Name scrambled: CRAFISN TOCST EYK

   Actual name: _____

7. In the middle of the night of August 24, 1814, this woman, risking her own safety, saved Stuart's portrait of Washington, a special copy of the Declaration of Independence, and the autographs of the signers.

   Name scrambled: YODLEL SNIMODA Actual name: _____

By now you should be ready to set up your own rogues' gallery or write a novel full of interesting people. Which will it be?

8
Mini-Mysteries

The time has come to put your know-how to good use. How many of the following "mysteries" can you solve?

Case A: The Confused Attorneys

Judge Adams glanced quickly over the records. "Hmmm," he said thoughtfully. Then he narrowed his eyes and looked over his glasses. "You're Tom Jones, the plaintiff?" he asked.

Jones nodded, a little fearfully.

The Judge looked a little to the left. "And you're Bill Jenkins, the defendant?"

Jenkins giggled nervously. "Yes, Your Honor."

Judge Adams picked up the papers. "It says here that the defendant claims that the plaintiff allowed his pigs to get into the sheep meadow and that this upset some newborn lambs. The defendant also claims that the plaintiff hit him on the head, stole three cherry pies, and dumped a pail of frogs into his well." He paused. "Am I reading this correctly?"

Jones and Jenkins nodded in unison.

"Then—case dismissed!" the Judge said crossly. "And before you two clowns come back into court, get yourselves lawyers who know the correct terminology!"

Why did Judge Adams dismiss the case?

Case B: The Simpering Seamstress

Selena, a seamstress in the village of Saludo, lost her gold needle on Monday. For two days the entire police force interrogated witnesses and hunted for clues. Late Wednesday night they found a large footprint under the kitchen window of Selena's house. They made a moulage of the footprint, and then checked the shoe size of every adult who lived in Saludo.

Howie Moore's shoe exactly fitted the mold. Howie, a widower, a hermit, and the only housepainter in Saludo, wore dirty, but newly patched, overalls and a blue work shirt.

They slipped the handcuffs on Howie and started to lead him away. "You cain't lock me up in no jail," he said sullenly. "I ain't never seen no gold needle. I ain't never seen no needle at all."

The police pushed him into the squad car. "That sews up the case!" they said triumphantly. "There are no holes in it now. We'll just stop at your place, Howie, and pick up Miss Selena's gold needle. Then we'll all go and have a nice chat with the judge!"

Why were the police so sure they'd find Selena's gold needle at Howie's place? How did Howie give himself away?

Case C: A Swarm of Suspects

Alice Davis had been killed Tuesday night at 10:30. Now five men who had been courting Alice were lined up before Chief Morgan's desk.

"You were all pretty jealous, so you all had a motive for killing Alice," the Chief grumbled, "and you were all there Tuesday night. That makes you all suspects. Now let's hear what each of you has to say."

He listened closely to all five men.

Ed's story: "I saw Alice at a quarter to nine. As usual, she was watching that big 25-inch color television she has. I just delivered the chair I had fixed for her and left. I was tired."

Jim's story: "It was a little before 10 when I saw Alice. She gave me a piece of apple pie just out of the oven, and we made a date for Saturday night."

Ike's story: "I was there at 10:15. I had the second cut of that pie—she told me you had the first one, Jim—and a glass of milk. We made a date for Sunday night. I was there for no more than 10 minutes."

Ozzie's story: "I guess I was the first one to see Alice that night. I took over a basket of apples. She wanted to bake a pie, she said, but she had blown a fuse. She had to wait until the electricity was turned on. That was about 8:30."

Joe's story: "Alice called me just after you left, Ozzie. Said her electricity was off and wondered if I could check it. I went over about nine. It wasn't anything much to put in a new fuse, and I had it working in no time. She had the pie all ready—just had to pop it into the oven."

When they had all finished, Chief Morgan smiled with satisfaction. "O.K. you four. You can go. But you—!" He pinned _ _ _ _ _ _ _ _ _ _ 's arms behind his back. "You're going nowhere. You're a murderer and a liar, too!"

Who murdered Alice? What lie that the murderer told turned into a trap?

Two. Word Families—and Friends

1 What's in a Name?

Have you ever wondered what life would be like if there were no names? Suppose *people* had no names. If you wanted to catch Pete's attention, you'd have to shout down the street, "Hey, you with the red shirt!" Inconvenient, no?

It would be at least as inconvenient if *things* had no names. Think of asking someone to go into the next four-walled section (a room), open the thing that slides out of the wooden thing (chest of drawers) under the thing you can see through or open (a window), and bring you two knitted things that go over the things that you walk on (socks)!

Yes, names *are* important.

I. Take *doors*, for example. All of your life you have opened and closed doors, but can you identify *doorjamb*, *lintel*, *sill*, and *transom* in the sketch below?

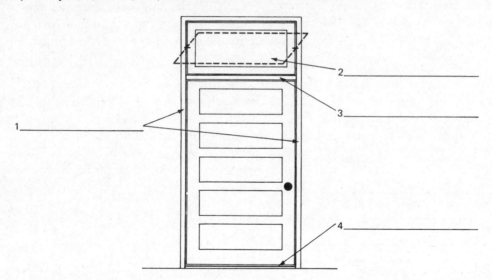

II. Take the *front* (or facade) of a *house*. You see dozens every day. Can you spot a *dormer*, *eaves*, a *bay window*?

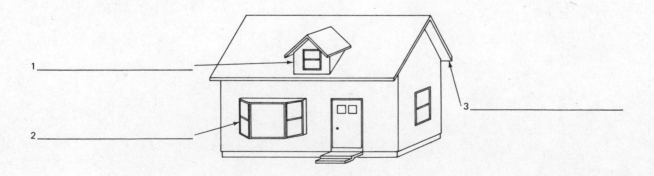

III. This time take some assorted *objects*—odd *o*nes. How many of the following can you identify? *Obelisk, ocarina, octagon, okra.* (If you are totally lost, check the definitions below the sketches, but first try to connect the names with the objects by using your deductive powers and the process of elimination.)

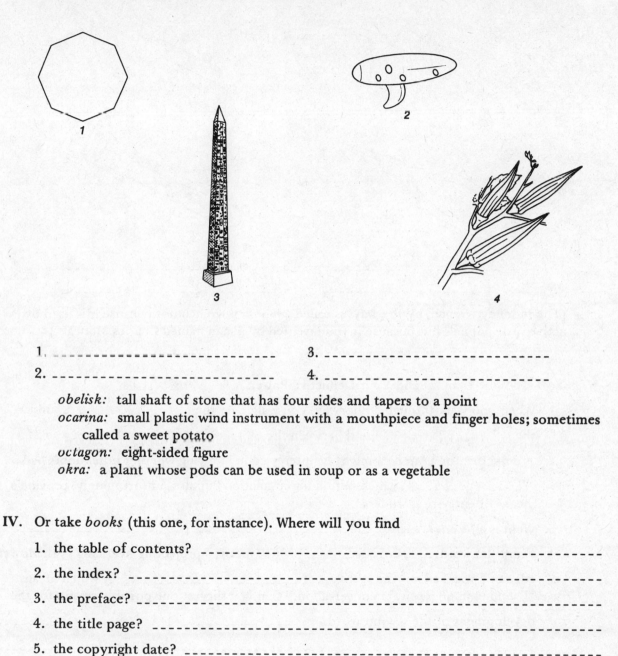

1. ---------------------------------- 3. ----------------------------------
2. ---------------------------------- 4. ----------------------------------

    obelisk: tall shaft of stone that has four sides and tapers to a point
    ocarina: small plastic wind instrument with a mouthpiece and finger holes; sometimes
        called a sweet potato
    octagon: eight-sided figure
    okra: a plant whose pods can be used in soup or as a vegetable

IV. Or take *books* (this one, for instance). Where will you find

1. the table of contents? --

2. the index? --

3. the preface? --

4. the title page? --

5. the copyright date? --

V. Take some ordinary *tools*, the kind that can be found in almost every household. Can you identify the *monkey wrench*, the *chisel*, the *pliers*, the *awl*?

1. _____   3. _____
2. _____   4. _____

(The monkey wrench, by the way, is called a *monkey* wrench not because it is used by active little animals but because it was invented by a man named Charles Moncke.)

VI. **To Test Your Memory and Your Deductive Powers**

1. When you walk through a doorway, you walk over the _____, under the _____ , and between the _____ .

2. A detective (or a burglar) might be interested in knowing whether hotel doors had _____ , which permit air circulation but also, unfortunately, provide a means of entry to intruders.

3. What is a *facade*? _____

4. From the word _____ , which means a projecting overhang at the lower edge of a roof, comes the word _____, which means "listening in on a private conversation." Can you suggest one possible reason for the development of the second word? _____

_____

5. Which one of the tools we named would be most efficient if you wished to

   a. pull a nail out of a piece of wood? _____

   b. sketch or etch a ship on a whale's tooth? _____

6. Would an *ocarina* or an *obelisk* be more suitable as a gift for a small boy?

_____

7. An *octagonal* house would have _ _ _ _ _ _ _ _ _ _ _ _ _ _ _ _ sides.

8. If you wish to create additional space in an attic, you can do so by adding a

   _ _ _ _ _ _ _ _ _ _ _ _ _ _ _ _ .

9. What is the difference between a *table of contents* and an *index*? _ _ _ _ _ _ _ _ _ _ _

   _

   _

   _

10. Without using the names of parts, describe the appearance and structure of a book.
    When you have finished writing, ask yourself if your description would make sense

    to someone who has never seen or heard of a book. _

    _

    _

    _

    _

    _

    _

Question: What's in a name?
Answer: Our entire ability to communicate!

2
Self: Outer View

I. Instructions

1. Take out a small pocket mirror. Then answer the questions in each group on the lines provided.

2. Study your *hair*. What color is it? Is it long or short, thick or thin, fine or coarse? Is it curly, wavy, or straight? Do you have a part? If so, where is it located? Do you have bangs? Any hair at all dipping down over the forehead? Do you wear it close to the head or fluffed out? Do you wear it forward on the face, as a frame, or pushed back?

----

3. Study your *forehead*. Consider its size, up and down. Is it a low forehead or a high forehead? Is it broad (i.e., does it extend far to the right and left)? Any wrinkles? If so, are they horizontal (left and right) or vertical (up and down)? Do you have a widow's peak (hairline coming to a V-shaped point in the middle of the forehead)? Does your hairline recede (go back) a bit at the part?

----

4. Study your *nose*. Is it long and thin, long and broad, short and thin, or short and broad? Is it a snub (short, turned-up) nose? Is it pointed? The bridge of a nose is the upper bony ridge that supports eyeglasses. From the bridge to the tip, is your nose arched, straight, or slightly concave (curving upward at the tip)?

----

5. Study your *lips*. Is your upper lip about the same length and breadth as your lower lip? Are your lips long or short? Full or thin? Do they droop a bit at the corners? Or do they turn up at the corners? Are they generally compressed (tight together)? What shade (of color) are they?

----

6. Study your *eyes*. Are they small, average, or large? Are they wide or narrow? What color are they? Are your eyelashes the same color as your hair or a different color? Are your eyelashes especially long or curly? Are your eyelids heavy? Are there little lines or deep lines at the corners of your eyes? Describe your eyes.

----

7. Study your *eyebrows*. Are they the same color as your hair or a different color? Are they thick or thin? Are they unruly (difficult to keep in order)? Do the inward edges line up with the sides of your nose? Or do your eyebrows almost meet above the bridge of your nose? Are they straight or arched? Are they thick at one side, thin at the other?

----

8. Study your *chin*. Is it square or round? Does it recede (slope backward) or jut forward? Is there a deep indentation above the chin but below the lower lip?

----

9. *Miscellaneous*. Are your cheeks full or thin? Do you have any birthmarks? Any scars? Do you have sideburns? A mustache? A beard? Are your ears close to your head? Do you wear glasses? If so, what kind? Do you have dimples? Where?

----

10. *Overall.* Is your face

▭ rectangular? ◯ oval? ◯ round? ▢ square?

What is your dominant (strongest) feature? Which feature do you think is memorable to a stranger meeting you for the first time?

II. Things to Do and Describe

1. Smile—as naturally as you can. How does a smile affect your lips, cheeks, jaw, eyes?

----

2. Laugh—again as naturally as you can. Which features are affected when you laugh? How?

----

3. Frown. What features are affected? How?

----

4. Raise your eyebrows. What features are affected? How?

----

5. Wink one eye. What features are affected? How?

III. **Now try these.**

Novelists often describe the appearance and movements of a character's eyes. Look in the mirror, and try to show the kind of eyes described in 1 to 7 below. Each time describe what you see.

1. Twinkling eyes: _

_ _

2. Sleepy eyes: _

_ _

3. Alert eyes: _

_ _

4. Glaring eyes: _

_ _

5. Shifty eyes: _

_ _

6. Blazing eyes: _

_ _

7. Dogged (stubborn) eyes: _

_ _

Do you have any conclusions about eye actions and their descriptions?

_ _

_ _

_ _

IV. **Activity**

Conjure up means "to bring into existence as if by magic." Now conjure up a memorable face, female or male. Keeping in mind the questions you answered about yourself, write a vivid and complete description of this memorable face. Don't try to include every detail; select those that will help a reader to "see" the face you are describing.

3
Self: Inner View

Now that you have taken a close outer view of yourself, how about attempting a close inner view? This is considerably more difficult. Few people have the courage to place *themselves* under a microscope. Do you?

The self-check below is personal. (Honesty is almost impossible if you know others are going to see your answers. For this reason we suggest you write the answers to this one section on a separate piece of paper.)

I. Self-Check

1. Are you *loquacious* (very talkative) or *reticent* (generally silent, reserved)?

    ----

2. Are you *arrogant* (overbearingly proud) or *humble* (modest, meek)?

    ----

3. Are you *absentminded* (forgetful, preoccupied) or *attentive* (observant, paying heed)?

    ----

4. Are you *amiable* (good-natured) or *sullen* (gloomy, sulky)? -----------------

5. Are you *naive* (childlike, simple) or *sophisticated* (worldly-wise)?

    ----

6. As a student, are you *diligent* (industrious) or *indolent* (lazy)? -----------------

7. Are you *candid* (frank, forthright) or *deceitful* (given to misrepresentation)?

    ----

8. In new situations, are you *timid* (fearful, hesitant) or *audacious* (bold, daring)?

    ----

9. When making decisions, are you *resolute* (firm, unyielding) or *vacillating* (wavering, changing sides)? -------------------------

10. About politics, are you *intense* (tending to feel deeply) or *apathetic* (uninterested, listless)? ----------------------

11. With money, are you *frugal* (thrifty) or *prodigal* (recklessly wasteful)?

    ----

12. With food, are you *abstemious* (moderate) or *gluttonous* (immoderate, tending to overindulge)? ---------------------

13. In an argument, are you *rational* (logical) or *irrational* (unreasonable, illogical)?

    ----

14. With an enemy, are you *merciless* (without mercy) or *compassionate* (sympathetic)?

    ----

15. In working with your hands, are you *awkward* (clumsy) or *dexterous* (skillful)?

II. To Test Your Memory

Write one of the italicized words above on each of the blanks below.

1. Benjy is so _____ that he will spend no more than 30 cents for his lunch.

2. After she was elected president of the student organization, she became so

   _____ that no one liked her.

3. The _____ professor dropped his spectacles into his tea and tried to put a sugar lump on his nose.

4. "Don't be lazy; be _____ ," said the teacher. "Do your homework—even if it means missing your favorite television program."

5. An _____ citizenry, more interested in ease and pleasure than in government, encourages corruption in its leaders.

6. He ate three sundaes, two sodas, and two banana splits. Then he asked if we thought

   he was _____ .

7. He was so _____ a fellow that children and pets, as well as adults, loved him.

8. She was so _____ that during our telephone conversation, I was able to read a chapter of a book and write a letter.

9. He changed his mind so often that they called him "_____ Vincent."

10. Her _____ delight at the bright lights and tall buildings of New York City charmed her more sophisticated escort.

III. To Test Your Deductive Powers

Think of a celebrity (real or fictitious) who seems to fit each of the following characteristics:

1. arrogant _____
2. frugal _____
3. compassionate _____
4. intense _____
5. audacious _____
6. loquacious _____
7. naive _____
8. sophisticated _____
9. rational _____
10. reticent _____

4
Clothes Make the Man (or Woman)!

"Good clothes open all doors." (proverb)

"I hate to see a man overdressed. . . . A man ought to look like he's put together by accident, not added up on purpose." (Christopher Morley, *Kitty Foyle*)

"Where's the man could ease a heart
Like a satin gown?"
(Dorothy Parker, "The Satin Dress")

"We are all Adam's children, but silk makes the difference." (proverb)

Do you choose your clothes for comfort? To reflect your own self-image? To attract others? Be careful! Your answer—like your clothing—will tell others something about you, just as their answers—and their clothing—can tell you something about them.

If clothes do not actually make the man, they do at least reflect his attitudes and values. That's reason enough for knowing a little about the "fashion game"!

I. Here are ten items of clothing. Begin your file on fashion by matching each item with its correct description.

bolero	cummerbund	pinafore
cardigan	dirndl	shift
cravat	knickers	tunic
culottes		

1. Little boys used to wear them. Golfers wear them. Girls and women wear them for play and sport. (*full breeches banded just below the knee*) _____

2. Little girls used to wear it. Now big girls wear it. (*a sleeveless dress, like an apron, often worn as an overdress*) _____

3. Tyrolean peasants used to wear it. For several decades girls have liked it. (*full-skirted dress with tight bodice*) _____

4. Both men and women wear it. A Spanish dance has the same name. A kind of dance music also has the same name. (*a short jacket with no front fastening*) _____

5. Both men and women wear it. A British army officer first made it popular. (*a sweater opening down the front*) _____

6. It was worn by both men and women in ancient Greece and Rome. It has been worn by soldiers in some armies. (*a long, loose-fitting garment, with or without sleeves, usually worn over a skirt or pants*) _____

7. They can be short, knee-length, or ankle-length. They are worn by women. (*full trousers that resemble a skirt*) _____

8. Originally it was worn in Persia. It is now worn by men at formal dances and other

affairs. In color, it varies. (*a broad pleated sash worn around the waist*)------------

----

9. Once it meant a shirt, then a nightgown. Now it refers to a woman's dress. (*a dress hanging straight from the shoulders*)--------------------

10. It was first worn by Croatian mercenaries hired by the French. It is now worn more often by men than women. (*a necktie*)--------------------

II. Next you should know some of the materials popular in the manufacture of clothes. Can you match the materials in the first column with the definitions in the second column? (Remember the process of elimination!)

---- 1. plaid
---- 2. corduroy
---- 3. jersey
---- 4. voile
---- 5. melton
---- 6. acrylic
---- 7. crepe
---- 8. tweed
---- 9. leather
---- 10. vinyl

a. a popular synthetic fiber

b. a flexible, shiny plastic

c. material having a pattern of rectangles formed by crossed lines of various widths

d. a coarse woolen fabric in a twill weave

e. a soft, light-weight knitted fabric

f. the tanned hide of an animal, with hair removed

g. a durable cotton fabric with vertical ribs

h. a smooth, heavy woolen cloth

i. a thin, soft fabric with a crinkled surface

j. a sheer fabric of cotton, silk, rayon, or wool

III. Keen observation and the ability to describe what we see are important skills—for the detective *and* the designer. Study each of the sketches below in the first column. Then, in the second column, answer each related question, emphasizing the italicized words.

1.

1. What is meant by a *chevron-striped* fabric? -----------

2.

2. What are *argyle* socks? -----------------------------

3.

3. What is a *mandarin* collar? _

_ _

_ _

4.

4. What is a *cowl* neckline? _

_ _

_ _

5.

5. What is a *voluminous* sleeve? _ _ _ _ _ _ _ _ _ _ _ _ _ _ _ _ _ _ _

_ _

_ _

IV. The last and very important information in your file is fashion *terminology*. If you know some of the terms related to clothing fashions, you can develop answers, through deduction, to all kinds of questions. Try these. When necessary, use a dictionary.

1. Fashion magazines talk about a *minimal wardrobe.* What is meant by this phrase, and

when would you be most interested in having one? _ _ _ _ _ _ _ _ _ _ _ _ _ _ _ _ _ _ _

_ _

_ _

_ _

2. White and pastels *reflect* light and heat, while darker colors *absorb* light and heat.

Which would you prefer in winter? In summer? Why? _ _ _ _ _ _ _ _ _ _ _ _ _ _ _ _ _ _ _

_ _

_ _

_ _

3. What is meant by a *color-coordinated* outfit? Why do some people consider this

coordination important? _

_ _

----

4. A shirtwaist dress or a button-down shirt is considered a *classic*. Why? - - - - - - - - -

----

----

5. There are *casual* clothes and *formal* clothes. Which would you wear to a barbecue? To

a prom? Define each term. -

----

6. If you say that a particular outfit is *chic*, are you being complimentary or critical?

How do you pronounce *chic*? -

----

7. It is often said that *accessories* make or break an outfit. How can they *make* it? How

can they *break* it? -

----

8. You are an ad writer. You are given two garments: a bright red cape with gold trim,
and a navy blue tailored suit to be worn with a white blouse. Which would you

describe as *dashing*? Which as *demure*? Give reasons for your choice. - - - - - - - - -

----

----

9. What exactly is an *appliquéd* leather-on-suede belt? What reason can you suggest for

the continuing popularity of *appliquéing*? -

----

10. If you are planning a six-months trip, which would you be most likely to buy—slacks made of a *crease-resistant* fabric or slacks made of a fabric with *high absorbency*?

Why? _____

_____

_____

_____

On the other hand—

"Better go to heaven in rags than to hell in embroidery." (proverb)

5
Eat to Live?
Or Live to Eat?

If you eat to live, you may be only mildly interested in what follows; but if you live to eat—ah, that's another story! Here's a chance to titillate (stimulate) your taste buds while you mix pralines (a crisp candy made of nut kernels and sugar syrup) and Perry Mason!

I. Who Am I?

chef   glutton   maitre d'
dietitian   gourmet

1. I am interested in your health—in the food and liquid that your body needs to operate efficiently. I count calories and watch vitamins and minerals. I am a _____.

2. I delight in the taste of food—in its quality, its texture, its beauty. I savor spices and exult in the exotic. I am a _____.

3. I love an abundance of food. Quality is for royalty; quantity is for me. A half dozen heroes is my idea of heaven! I am a _____.

4. I prepare food. I am a kitchen artist, and the dinner plate is my easel. To those who dine, I'm divine. I am a _____.

5. I supervise the serving of food. I guarantee polished silver and swift service. My staff sees that your drinks are cold and your rolls hot. I am a _____.

II. What Am I?

chowder   parfait   soufflé
croquette   petit four

1. I am an entrée (main dish) or a dessert. I am light and fluffy, baked of egg yolk and beaten egg whites. My main ingredient may be salmon or strawberries. I am a _____.

2. I am a thick soup containing clams or bits of other fish. Sometimes I have a milk base. I am especially popular in New England. I am a _____.

3. I am a small, square tea cake. I am completely covered with frosting. Sometimes I am decorated. I am a _____.

4. I am a cone-shaped mass of minced chicken or shrimp. I am usually covered with bread crumbs before being deep-fried. I am a _____.

5. I am a dessert. I am a mixture of cream and sugar, eggs and flavoring. I am frozen and served in a tall glass. Lately I have been just several layers of ice cream served with a sauce. I am a _____.

III. Around the World

> chili con carne   pizza   shish kebab
> chop suey   sauerbraten

1. I am Chinese-American. I am a combination of small pieces of meat and vegetables. Usually I am served with rice. I am _____ .

2. I am Italian-American. I have a shallow crust, and I am filled with tomato, cheese, and spice. I am baked. I am a _____ .

3. I am Turkish-American. I am chunks of meat and tomato and onion, usually highly seasoned. I am served on a skewer. I am _____ .

4. I am Spanish-American. I am a "hot" combination of meat, beans, and powdered or minced peppers. I am drowned in spices. I am _____ .

5. I am German-American. I am beef marinated in vinegar and spices before being cooked. I am usually served with dumplings and red cabbage. I am _____ .

IV. Egg Hunt

An egg is oval and thin-shelled, with a yellow yolk and white albumen. Sounds simple, doesn't it? But an egg is versatile (has many abilities and uses). Watch!

First, you can cook an egg. You can

_____ it—that is, cook it in hot fat;

or _____ it—cook it in the shell in very hot water;

or _____ it—cook it out of the shell in boiling water;

or _____ it—beat it up and cook it in hot fat.

You can also
beat it up, cook it, and fold it around ham, cheese, or onion and have a(n) _____ ,

or

poach it, place it on toast and ham, cover it with hollandaise sauce, and have _____ .

Second, you can add letters and create new words.

egg_____ —a widely cultivated plant, the fruit of which has a dark, glossy purple skin and is eaten as a vegetable

egg_____ —a drink consisting of beaten eggs and milk, and sometimes rum

egg_____ —a kitchen utensil that is excellent for whipping cream egg _ _ _ _ _ —a Chinese-American favorite, an egg pastry wrapped around seafood or minced vegetables and fried

Third, you can resort to slang and say

that a nice fellow is a _ _ _ _ _ egg,

that the performer who failed so completely _ _ _ _ _ an egg,

that an intellectual is an egg_ _ _ _ _ .

Fourth, you can grow philosophical and develop proverbs:

Robespierre said: "Omelets are not made without <u>b</u>_ _ _ _ _ _ _ _ eggs."

J. P. Morgan said: "Can you <u>u</u>_ _ _ _ _ _ _ _ _ _ eggs?"

An old proverb says: "Don't put all your eggs <u>i</u> _ <u>o</u> _ _ <u>b</u> _ _ _ _ _ ."

V. Activity

Reread the three quotations immediately above. What would happen in each case if you substituted *turnips* for *eggs*? Why is the word *eggs* a more logical and appropriate choice?

6
A House Is Not a Home . . .

First there was a cave . . . then, perhaps, a tree house . . . and now a high-rise apartment. In between were all sorts of structures (buildings) in which people found shelter from storm, sun, and wind.

I. How many of the structures in the first column can you match with the definitions in the second column?

---- 1. igloo

---- 2. tepee

---- 3. sod hut

---- 4. bungalow

---- 5. penthouse

---- 6. tenement

---- 7. ranch

---- 8. mansion

---- 9. chateau

---- 10. chalet

a. an apartment on the top floor or roof of a building

b. a large, stately house

c. a house built of blocks of snow

d. a small house, with sloping roof, seen in Alpine areas

e. a dwelling made of clumps of grass-covered soil

f. a large farm on which cattle and horses are raised; today, also a low suburban house

g. a cone-shaped tent of skin or bark

h. a building, especially in the poorer part of the city, with quarters for many families

i. a one-story house with a low-pitched roof

j. a large country house or castle in France

II. Ready for some detective work? Fine! Here are a few more places in which people live.

barracks   parsonage   sanatorium
dormitory   penitentiary   studio
monastery

Your job is to find the following persons. In which of the places above would you be most likely to find each one?

1. This man is a clergyman and is in charge of a parish. _____

2. This young fellow is a private in the United States Army. _____

3. This woman is an artist. She does most of her painting in her own apartment. _____

_____

4. This young girl is attending a college that is over 200 miles from her family home.

_____

5. This man was tried, found guilty, and sentenced to 99 years in prison. _____

_____

6. This man is a monk, living under religious vows. _____

7. This young girl has tuberculosis and needs regular medical supervision. _ _ _ _ _ _ _ _ _ _ _ _
_ _ _ _ _ _ _ _ _ _ _

III. But that was yesterday. Today the emphasis is on new kinds of living. Have you heard of a
leisure village?
condominium?
cooperative?
commune?

Sharpen your deductive powers by deciding how the four terms above should be distributed into the four blanks below.

A young man who wants to participate in group living, to share his life with others, may choose to live in a (1) _ . A senior citizen who has retired and has time for sports and hobbies may choose a (2) _ . The young couple who would like to associate with others in joint ownership and operation of an apartment house may choose a (3) _ . And the older couple who wish to own, not rent, but are tired of gardening, painting, and other responsibilities may choose to buy a single apartment, or a (4) _ , in a house operated by a managerial staff.

IV. Change roles now. Play city manager for a while. Your assignment is to establish a *planned community*, one that will be more comfortable, more beautiful, more interesting than the older unplanned towns and cities. The following questions pose typical problems. Be sure you have a good reason for each answer. Then turn to the end of the exercise and compare your answers with those of the experts.

1. Would you install mail slots in front doors or group mailboxes at regular intervals?

_ _

2. Would you design a "precise roadway grid"

or curved roads leading to "oval cul-de-sacs"?

3. How would you avoid having an "overhead lattice" (open framework, often criss-

crossing) of utility lines from poles? _____

_____

4. Would you program "homogeneous rows of single-family houses" or a mixture of

   different kinds of single-family houses with garden apartments and townhouses? _____

   _____

5. Would you restrict the population of the village to 5,000, 15,000, 50,000, or 150,000?

   _____

6. Which of the following would you consider essential for a well-organized village? (You
   may choose as many or as few as you wish.) Plazas; meeting halls; shops; distinct

   neighborhoods *within* the village, each with its own grade school. _____

   _____

7. Would you permit (*a*) billboards, (*b*) TV aerials? _____

8. Would you encourage or discourage gripe sessions? Why? _____

   _____

   The questions above and the following answers are based largely on an article in the
New York Times (Dec. 26, 1971) about James W. Rouse, who in the 1960's built the
planned community of Columbia, Maryland.

Answers

1. group mailboxes
2. curved roads on oval cul-de-sacs
3. by placing all such lines underground
4. mixture rather than one type only
5. 15,000
6. all of these
7. neither
8. encourage in order to stimulate involvement

V. To Test Your Memory

1. What is a *planned community*? _____

   _____

2. In what part of the world would you expect to find a *chalet*? _____

   _____

3. What type of house bears a name formerly used only to denote a cattle farm? _____

   _____

4. Communal living means _____ living.

5. What is the difference between a *condominium* and a *cooperative*? ------------------

----

VI. To Test Your Deductive Powers

1. What seems to be the current trend regarding living quarters for the different generations? ---

----

2. Which are more conducive (contributory) to a relaxed environment: straight lines or curved lines? ----------------------------------

3. What relationship exists between the kind of house built and the region and historical age in which it is built? --

----

----

4. What does the word *homogeneous* mean? ------------------

5. In addition to the trend mentioned in question #1, what other trend seems to exist in this country today? (Clue: Consider the types of housing named in Section I and compare them with those named in Section III.) ------------------------------

----

7
School Bells Ring

When it comes to schools, *you* are the expert! You have probably (and more than once) wailed, "If *I* had anything to say about it, schools would be different!" Well, jump on Cloud 99! Here's your chance to design a blueprint* for your very own ideal school!

I. First, become a curriculum specialist. Do you understand what kind of information and skills are offered in all these courses?

accounting	geometry
biology	journalism
ceramics	physics
foreign languages	political science
geology	retailing

(If you do, you should be able to give advice to the following students. If you do not, you should still be able to do so after you check the clues: roots, related words, the process of elimination.)

1. Bill wants to be a reporter. He should study _____ .

2. Jean is fascinated by the rocks that make up the earth's structure. She should study

_____ .

3. Frank hopes to become a doctor. He needs some knowledge of the way living creatures function and grow. He should study _____ .

4. Marie is interested in measurement, especially in the rules governing surfaces, angles, etc., found on earth. She should study _____ .

5. Jack is interested in matter and energy and such subjects as motion and light. He should study _____ .

6. Rae likes to make things out of clay, and she has some artistic ability. She should study _____ .

7. Vic would like to be able to keep the financial records for his family's small sporting-goods store. He should study _____ .

8. Phil's family also owns a store. He plans to work as a salesman after his graduation. He should study _____ .

9. Chris dreams of becoming a Senator. She should study _____ .

10. Larry thinks he would like to work as an interpreter at the United Nations. He should study _____ .

*A blueprint is a photographic copy (white lines on blue paper) of architectural plans.

II. Second, become an expert in educational philosophy.

1. Do you approve of *homogeneous* grouping (grouping individuals of similar ability) or *heterogeneous* grouping (grouping individuals of varying ability)? _ _ _ _ _ _ _ _ _ _ _ _ _ _
_ _ _ _ _ _ _ _ _ _

2. Should *individualized instruction* (instruction different for each student) be a regular part of the school day? _ _ _ _ _

3. Should students be able to pursue *independent study* (study by oneself, with a minimum of supervision)? _ _ _ _ _

4. Will *tutorials* (classes for a few students working with a teacher) exist? _ _ _ _ _ _
Seminars (small discussion groups)? _ _ _ _ _

5. What student-teacher *ratio* (number of students per teacher) would you prefer?
_ _ _ _ _ _ _ _

6. Do you approve of *programmed instruction* (step-by-step learning, predesigned)? If so, would you have it used by all students or only by some students? _ _ _ _ _ _ _ _ _ _ _ _ _ _ _
_ _ _ _ _ _ _ _ _ _ _ _ _ _ _ _ _ _

7. Would you retain the present *eggcrate schedule* (all classes meet every day at the same time for the same length of time) or try for a *modular schedule* (classes meet on different days for varying lengths of time)? _

8. Would any subjects be required, or would all be *electives* (courses freely chosen by the students)? If the former, which subjects would be required and for how long?
_ _
_ _

9. What would be the maximum number of students registered in an ideal school?
_ _ _ _ _ _ _ _ _ _

10. Should students be in school only when they have classes (college method) or all day?
_ _

III. Third, become a school architect.

1. Would the school building be one, two, or three stories? _ _ _ _ _ _

2. What size classroom would you propose? (This will depend on your educational philosophy.) How many classrooms would you need for your proposed maximum student population? _
_ _

3. Would you include *learning centers* (areas where students can work individually)? If so,

how many? Where would they be located? _____

_____

4. Where would the gymnasium be? _____

the cafeteria? _____

the library? _____

the administrative suite? _____

the clinic (or health office)? _____

the teachers' lounge? _____

5. Would there be a students' lounge? If so, where? _____

_____

6. Would there be *curriculum centers* (areas providing materials helpful in revising or

developing courses of study)? If so, where? _____

_____

7. What areas not already mentioned would you include? _____

_____

Do you *still* feel like an expert on modern schools?

IV. **To Test Your Deductive Powers**

1. What is the difference between *individualized instruction* and *independent study*?

_____

_____

_____

2. What is the difference between *homogeneous* and *heterogeneous* groups? _____

_____

_____

3. What does the word element *geo* mean? _____

4. How does type of instruction affect desirable classroom size? _____

_____

_____

_____

5. What does *curriculum* mean? _____

_____

6. Blueprints are most commonly used by members of what profession? _ _ _ _ _ _ _ _ _ _ _ _
_ _ _ _ _ _ _ _ _ _

7. Why do you suppose that a schedule that calls for all classes to meet every day at the same time for the same length of time is known as an *eggcrate schedule*? _ _ _ _ _ _ _ _ _ _
_ _
_ _
_ _

8. *Innovation* means a change, a new approach. What innovation would you most like to try in your present school? _
_ _
_ _

9. If you are invited to attend a *seminar* on women's rights, sponsored by a local church, what kind of meeting would you expect it to be? _
_ _
_ _

10. Would a school that used most of the innovative approaches mentioned in this chapter be easier or more difficult to operate than a traditional school? Give reasons for your answer. _
_ _
_ _
_ _

8
Seven-League Boots

In 1892 Nellie Bly set a record by going around the world in 72 days, 6 hours, and 11 minutes. Today *you* are going around the world—in about 20 minutes!
Ready?

I. You will start in a moment, but before you do, you will want to know a few terms essential to every traveler. See how many of these terms you can match with their definitions.

```
____  1. passport          a. a book of maps

____  2. visa              b. a hotel rate including meals as well as room

____  3. customs           c. lodgings; room and food

____  4. reservations      d. a certificate of identity and citizenship and of permission
                              to travel abroad
____  5. itinerary
                           e. place where baggage is inspected when one enters a
____  6. atlas                country

____  7. gazetteer         f. accommodations secured in advance

____  8. accommodations    g. tips for service

____  9. gratuities        h. a proposed route for a journey

____ 10. American plan     i. an official authorization on a passport permitting entry
                              into a particular country

                           j. a geographical dictionary
```

II. Now that everything's in order, you will want to take a look at the world you're going to see. Here is an illustrated map. Inspect it.

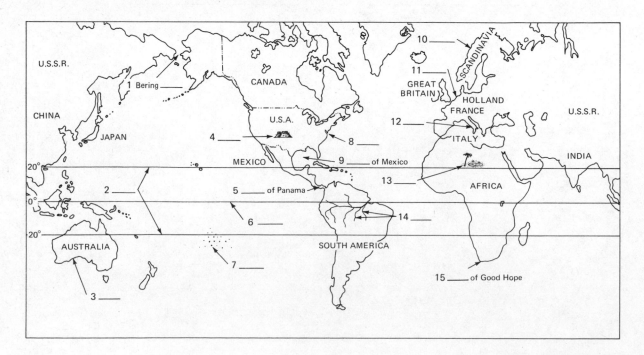

Below are the definitions of some terms. Read them, understand them, then write the letter of each term in the appropriate blank on the map.

a. *gulf:* a large area of sea partly surrounded by land
b. *peninsula:* a long piece of land that is connected to the mainland but juts out into the sea
c. *tributaries:* smaller rivers that flow into a large river
d. *strait:* a narrow passage of water that connects two larger bodies of water
e. *island:* land completely surrounded by water
f. *isthmus:* a narrow strip of land connecting two larger pieces of land
g. *cape:* a point of land jutting out into the sea
h. *archipelago:* a large group of small islands
i. *inlet:* a stream leading inland from the sea
j. *latitude:* distance north or south of the equator
k. *equator:* the circle around the center of the earth
l. *oasis:* a fertile spot, one having water, in a desert. The desert is marked on the map by a palm tree and a pool of water.
m. *fjord:* a narrow, deep inlet between steep cliffs
n. *mesa:* a flat-topped elevation with clifflike sides
o. *dike:* a low wall of earth or rock built to hold back water

III. You are now on your way. Your itinerary includes

France	Japan
Great Britain	Mexico
Holland	Scandinavia
India	United States
Italy	U.S.S.R.

At each stop the country being visited is described briefly and its monetary unit (basic kind of money) given. From these clues, deduce the name of the country or area you are in at each stop.

1. This is an island separated from Europe by a channel. It was the home of Shakespeare. It is a monarchy, currently ruled by a queen. Its monetary unit is the pound. Its name

   is _ .

2. This is a coastal country bounded on the west by the Atlantic Ocean. It is the home of fashion designers, perfume manufacturers, and gourmets. Its monetary unit is the

   franc. Its name is _ .

3. This is a group of countries sometimes called the land of the "midnight sun." The Norsemen lived here centuries ago. It has great fjords. Its monetary unit is the krone,

   or krona. Its name is _ .

4. This country is filled with canals that often rise above the level of the land. For this reason the people have built many dikes. It is also known for its tulips and wooden

   shoes. Its monetary unit is the guilder. Its name is _ .

5. This country is a peninsula bounded on the south by the Mediterranean Sea. It is

known for its ancient ruins and art treasures. Its monetary unit is the lira. Its name is _____ .

6. This is a huge country known for its borscht (beet soup) and for its devotion to Lenin's ideas. Its symbol is the great bear. Its monetary unit is the ruble. Its name is _____ .

7. This country has the largest agricultural population in the world. Famous are the Taj Mahal, the gurus, and the reverence for cows. Its monetary unit is the rupee. Its name is _____ .

8. This is a small island country, but it has become a great industrial nation. It is known for its production of cameras and Toyotas. Its monetary unit is the yen. Its name is

_____ .

9. This country is the southern neighbor of the United States. It has famous resort areas. Some of its national dishes—tamales, chilis, and enchiladas—are enjoyed by the people of other lands. Its monetary unit is the peso. Its name is _____ .

10. This country has mesas in the Southwest and numerous inlets along its Eastern coast. It has landed men on the moon! Its monetary unit is the dollar. Its name is

_____ .

Home—safe and sound!

IV. To Test Your Deductive Powers

Here are seven words used geographically in the preceding text. In the sentences that follow, they are used in a different way. See if you can insert each into the appropriate blank.

dike	itinerant	passport
gulf	oasis	peninsula
island		

1. A(n) _____ worker would be one who travels from place to place.

2. The two ambitious sisters were separated by a(n) _____ of suspicion and misunderstanding.

3. The only _____ in the otherwise barren day was the hour I spent in the library.

4. Cyrano de Bergerac described his extraordinarily long nose as a(n) _____ because it jutted out from his face.

5. "No man is a(n) _____ ," said the poet John Donne, meaning that no one can be totally separated from other human beings.

6. "This is my _____ to happiness!" said Sue, as she held up her letter of acceptance from Yale University.

7. Price control is one method of building a(n) _____ against the flood-waters of inflation.

9
Midget Mysteries

Recently Detective O'Hara had a hard day. Within eight hours he had to solve eight mysteries. Fortunately he caught the clue word or words in each case and solved all of them. How many can you solve?

1. Detective O'Hara: "Where were you on the night of December 16th?"

   Suspect Jones: "I couldn't have committed the murder here in New York that night. I was traveling on the Dutch peninsula."

   How did Detective O'Hara know that Jones was lying?

   ----

2. A young man who wished to be a detective told O'Hara that he had solved the Schneider burglary. "I checked the ground just three feet under the dormer window in the Schneiders' house," he announced, "and found Fred Wilson's footprints there. Obviously he's the burglar!"

   Why did Detective O'Hara decide that the young man was not bright enough to emulate (imitate) Sherlock Holmes?

   ----

3. "I saw the criminal clearly," said Miss Bryan. "He had oval eyes that were very round, and he had a widow's peak. He had a large birthmark on the lower part of his chin. And he was almost completely bald. And, oh yes, he had a long, heavy beard."

   Detective O'Hara laughed and said he couldn't use her as a witness. Why?

   ----

4. Dick R. was a glutton; Jim X. was abstemious. On Friday night one of them broke into the Large Scoop Ice Cream Shoppe and stole $53, three tubs of ice cream, a pound of walnuts, a jar of chocolate syrup, and a pint of strawberries. On the counter were three dishes that had apparently been filled with ice cream. They were now empty.

   Which one of the two suspects did O'Hara arrest? Why?

   ----

5. "You can't hold me!" Bert said with hostility. "I had nothing to do with the robbery of the old man."

   "But you did give shelter to the criminal afterward, didn't you?"

   "Yes."

"And you hid the money and the watch he had stolen?"

"Yes."

"Then you're an accessory after the fact," said O'Hara, "and I most certainly can hold you!"

What did O'Hara mean?

----

6. Detective O'Hara and the suspect, Bix Bones, looked at the objects spread out on the desk. They had all come from Bix's pockets. They included a flashlight, a pair of pliers, an awl, a wrench, and two handkerchiefs.

"You see," Bix protested. "I couldn't have stabbed that girl. I had no weapon—no knife, no ice pick, nothing. How could I have done it?"

"With this!" said O'Hara, picking up one of the objects as he booked Bones for murder. What did O'Hara pick up? Why could it have been used as a weapon?

----

7. "So you found my fingerprints on the cash register," cried Sally Perkins. "You still can't arrest me. If I took the money, where did I hide it? You've searched the whole house!"

O'Hara looked at Sally's high school record. She was studying English, social studies, ceramics, biology, and algebra. Then he looked around the room. He picked up a large hollow ball made of unfired clay. "The money is in here," he declared. When he broke it open, he found the missing $323.

What made O'Hara break the ball?

----

8. Sly Will was versatile. He had worked as an extra in the Tarzan movies, as a sailor, as a cross-country truck driver, and most recently as a tennis instructor. Now it looked as though he had committed a murder. But how could the police prove it? O'Hara kept remembering what Sly Will had said.

"Look, copper, you know I have an alibi. I was in my own penthouse apartment, and one of your men was outside my door. The girl was killed in an apartment across the alley, one story below. How could I have stabbed her?"

It was true. Yet O'Hara was sure that somehow Sly Will had done just that.

O'Hara tried to relax a bit as the music of his son's ocarina filled the police station. Tommy was playing "The Man on the Flying Trapeze." Suddenly O'Hara grinned. "Of course! That's how he did it!"

He took a half-dollar from his pocket and flipped it to Tommy. "Here, son, get yourself a slice of pizza! You've just helped me to solve a real puzzler!"

How did Tommy help his father to solve this mystery? How could Sly Will have killed the girl?

Three. Words to Tickle the Funny Bone

1
Laugh-in

"Laughter is the joyous, universal evergreen of life," Abraham Lincoln once said. What he meant, surely, is that laughter, like the evergreen, is alive in all seasons.

What is this thing called laughter?

An infant laughs; yet laughter is not simple.

A fool laughs; yet laughter requires intelligence.

Laughter ends; yet it does not die.

What, then, is laughter?

I. A. First, it is a thing we *do*. We laugh in different ways at different things. Here are five ways we laugh.

cackle   giggle   snort
chuckle   guffaw

How many can you match with their definitions?

1. We laugh in a high-pitched voice and with repeated short catches of breath. We

   _____ .

2. We laugh noisily or coarsely. We _____ .

3. We laugh with one loud outburst of scorn. We _____ .

4. We laugh inwardly or quietly. We _____ .

5. We laugh in a sharp, broken way (sounding like a hen). We _____ .

B. We can also change the sound of laughter by changing adjectives. Use a dictionary to explain the difference between

1. a *derisive* laugh and a *tolerant* laugh _____

   _____

   _____

2. a *sarcastic* laugh and a *gleeful* laugh _____

   _____

   _____

II. Second, we laugh at *things*. We laugh at (a)

burlesque   farce   parody
comic book   impersonation   satire
comic opera   pantomime   vaudeville
comic strip

Can you match these with their definitions?

1. a play characterized by extreme improbability of plot (story line), intended to make people laugh ---------------------------

2. a musical dramatic work of an amusing nature ---------------------------

3. a piece of writing that ridicules an author's style by imitating it -----------------------------

4. a dramatic presentation that ridicules a subject by treating it incongruously* ----------------------------

5. a series of cartoons that tells a story or carries a situation forward -------------------------

6. a light theatrical entertainment featuring songs, dances, and comic acts ----------------------------

7. a performance in which the actors use few or no words ----------------------

8. a booklet of comic strips, sometimes humorous, sometimes violent -------------------------

9. the art of imitating someone else's speech and actions ------------------------

10. a literary work in which sharp ridicule is used to expose and discredit evil ----------------------

III. We laugh at some *short things*, too . . . at a(n)

anecdote	gag	riddle
epigram	pun	tall story

This time try to match each term with one of the "samples" given below.

1. "Why does a chicken cross the road?"

    "To get to the other side!"   1. ----------------------

2. Teacher to student William, who complained that he could not finish his homework:

    "Where there's a Will, there's a way!"   2. ----------------------

3. "When I am dead, I hope it may be said:
    His sins were scarlet—but his books were read."

             "On His Books"—Hilaire Belloc   3. ----------------------

Incongruous is the most important word in the vocabulary of comedy. It means "inappropriate," "not logical," "out of place." Treating the theft of a needle as a major crime is incongruous, hence funny (*Gammer Gurton's Needle*). Treating the poisoning of a group of people flippantly is incongruous, hence funny (*Arsenic and Old Lace*). Almost everything that makes us laugh has some element of incongruity.

4. Paul Bunyan grew grapes so big that he was able to squeeze a glassful of juice from each of them.

4. _____

5. I couldn't commit suicide if my life depended on it.

5. _____

6. When the great Winston Churchill once took a young woman in to dinner (according to the novelist Gertrude Atherton), she said boldly that there were two things she didn't like about him. He asked her what they were, and she replied: "Your new politics and your mustache." Courteously Churchill retorted: "My dear madam, pray do not disturb yourself. You are not likely to come in contact with either."

6. _____

IV. Activities

Demonstrate the infectious (tending to spread easily) nature of laughter. If a record of laughter is available, play it in class—and watch what happens! If such a record is not available, one or two students should begin laughing as loudly as they can.

After the infectious nature of laughter has been demonstrated, consider these questions:

1. Why do so many TV shows use "canned" laughter?

2. Why do you feel self-conscious watching a comedy in a movie theater where only a few people are present?

3. Do people watching a comedy on TV and people watching a film in a crowded theater react in the same way?

4. How does a live audience affect a comedian's act? Could his act be good one day and only passable the next *because* of different audience reactions?

2
Riddles and Puns

Riddles and puns have one thing in common: they drive people crazy. Twelve-year-olds are especially susceptible to (liable to be stricken by) riddle-addiction, while intellectuals favor puns. In fact, the young riddle-addict often grows up to be a pun-addict. Whether that's a promise or a threat depends on your point of view!

A riddle, according to the *American Heritage Dictionary*, is "a question or statement requiring thought to answer or understand . . . something perplexing; an enigma."

An example (one of President Lincoln's favorites):

> Q. "If there are three pigeons sitting on a fence and you shoot one of them, how many are left?"
>
> A. "None—the other two will fly away!"

A pun, according to the same august, awe-inspiring authority, is "a play on words, sometimes on different senses of the same word and sometimes on the similar sense or sound of different words."

An example of the first type:

> "It's easy to see through people who make spectacles of themselves." (Thomas A. Lahey, C.S.C.)

An example of the second type:

> "They went and told the sexton
> And the sexton tolled the bell."
>   (Thomas Hood)

Punning—both making and appreciating puns—is more difficult because you must have a really good knowledge and understanding of words. In the first example, there is no fun if you do not realize that *spectacles* has two meanings: (1) eyeglasses, i.e., things through which we see; and (2) objects of curiosity, especially strange objects! In the second example, you will miss the fun if you do not know the meaning of *tolled* ("rang" or "sounded").

Ready to be challenged? Here are quite a few riddles, puns, and pun-riddles. Tackle them and try for a touchdown!

I. These are very easy pun-riddles based on proper names that have an independent meaning. You have only to look around the class to find each answer. Then explain each briefly.

> *Example:*
> Q. Who wins every race?
> A. Victor. (The name Victor also means "winner" or "conqueror.")

1. Q. Who has the most money?

    A. _____

2. Q. Who is a beam of light?

    A. _____

3. Q. Who is red or white and a June-bloomer?

    A. _____

4. Q. Who is a coin of little value?

A. _____

5. Q. Who is equipped with a common burglar's tool?

A. _____

6. Q. Who is always candid and honest?

A. _____

II. The second group is a little harder. Each question is followed by an incomplete quotation. By inserting appropriate words that rhyme with the missing words of the original quotations, you can find the solutions to these riddles.

> *Example:*
> Q. What does an annoyed nonsmoker say when someone lights a cigarette?
> A. Where there's smoke, there's _____."
> (*Ire.* It rhymes with *fire* and means "anger.")

A list of the original quotations used below appears at the end of this chapter. Consult it *only* if you find it necessary. Ready?

1. Q. What does a mother say to her small son on Easter morning?

A. "A fool and his _____ are soon parted!"

2. Q. What does a store manager say to a still unsatisfied customer?

A. "If at first you don't succeed, _____ , _____ again!"

3. Q. What might you say to a weight-conscious glutton who is devouring everything in sight?

A. "Haste makes _____ !"

4. Q. What did the frightened tree say to the sorceress during the forest fire?

A. "A _____ in time saves _____ !"

5. Q. What does the tailor say to his scholarly apprentice?

A. "Too many _____ spoil the _____ !"

III. This last group is a potpourri (a mixture; a collection). It includes all kinds of pun-riddles. In each case some clues are given: a partial answer or the number of letters needed. Use your deductive ability, and see how many of these you can solve.

1. Q. When is a prosecuting attorney most irritable?

A. When he is involved in a _____ examination!

2. Q. What did the female forger say to her apprentice?

A. _____ on!

3. Q. What did the seamstress say to the heckler?

A. Don't _____ me!

4. *Q.* Teacher: What is the longest sentence in the world?

   A. Reformed thief: _ _ _ _ _ !

5. *Q.* What did the bride say when she saw the honeymoon suite?

   A. How _ _ _ _ _ _ _ _ it is!

6. *Q.* Why doesn't a belligerent little boy need crayons when he wants to draw?

   A. Because he uses his _ _ _ _ _ _ _ !

7. *Q.* Is life worth living?

   A. That depends upon the _ _ _ _ _ _ _ !

8. *Q.* Why is a certain grain like a crooked smile?

   A. Because it's _ _ _ _ _ _ _ !

9. *Q.* How does a window resemble a small boy who has eaten green apples?

   A. They both have a _ _ _ _ _ _ _ in the middle!

10. *Q.* When is a pretty girl like an inept archer?

    A. When she has difficulty handling a _ _ _ _ _ _ _ !

11. *Q.* Why is an artist like a cowboy?

    A. They're both quick on the _ _ _ _ _ _ _ !

12. *Q.* First cannibal: "Shall we roast the minister?"

    A. Second cannibal: "Of course not. He's a _ _ _ _ _ _ _ !"

13. *Q.* Why is a magnate like a magnet?

    A. Because he attracts _ _ _ _ _ _ _ !

14. *Q.* Why is a baker like a hobo?

    A. He _ _ _ _ _ _ _ a little dough!

And last, but not least:

15. *Q.* What did Sir James Barrie, the author of *Peter Pan*, say to the critic who asked him if all his plays were successful?

    A. "Some _ _ _ _ _ _ _ out and some _ _ _ _ _ _ _ out!"

IV. Activity

Devise (invent) two pun-riddles of your own. Test them on your friends. If the class comes up with some really good ones, you may wish to write them down, type them, and distribute them. You may even sell a few copies for a penny each. Then you can truly say that a pun is sweet because it's a scent!

Original Quotations
1. A fool and his money are soon parted.
2. If at first you don't succeed, try, try again.
3. Haste makes waste.
4. A stitch in time saves nine.
5. Too many cooks spoil the broth.

3
Pedantry Prevails

If you say, "Put out the light," that's straightforward English.

If you say, "Extinguish the illumination," that's gobbledegook!

Gobbledegook is language that is too wordy, too technical, and too indirect. You will find it in government reports, in contracts, and in business and professional journals. It sounds intelligent, but it's really just pedantic (bookish and rule-ridden)!

Even so, playing with gobbledegook can be fun. Translating it is a little like breaking a code.

Suppose someone saunters up to you and says, "If one desires to urge upon another a general compliance with a specific principle, one ought to observe, scrupulously and habitually, that same principle." What would you reply? For that matter, what did the speaker say?

If you use your dictionary and that detective sense you have been developing, you should be able to translate the first half of the sentence (up to "specific principle") as "If you want to preach," and the rest of the sentence as "practice." Put these together and you have

"Practice what you preach."

Easy, isn't it?

I. Here are five examples of gobbledegook versions of well-known proverbs. With the help of a dictionary, try to find the original proverbs.

1. One is not able to retain possession of a sweet-tasting baked product and simultaneously consume said product.

----

2. Canines uttering hard, abrupt sounds do not simultaneously pierce someone's epidermis with the hard, bonelike structures rooted in their jaws.

----

3. Any human being who is afflicted with great physical, mental, or emotional pain has an intense fondness and preference for association with others who are similarly afflicted.

----

4. Before one considers acting precipitately, as if springing from the ground, one should obtain visual knowledge of the environment and any circumstances affecting it.

----

5. Participate in the creation and expression of affection and benevolence, not of belligerence and martial confrontation.

II. Now reverse the procedure and turn these five proverbs into gobbledegook. Good luck!

1. The early bird catches the worm.

_____

_____

2. Variety is the spice of life.

_____

_____

_____

3. A watched pot never boils.

_____

_____

_____

4. Necessity is the mother of invention.

_____

_____

_____

5. Spare the rod and spoil the child.

_____

_____

_____

Wasn't that a genial and pleasant diversion—to wit, *fun*?

4

Pop Poetry

Yesterday children sang nursery songs. Today a different generation of children chants TV commercials. Either way the emphasis is on *rhyme*.

Rhyme is as natural, as infectious, as whistling or humming or tapping one's foot to mark a musical beat.

So roll out your rhyme sense. It's

RHYME TIME!

I. The following couplets are not quite complete. See if you can finish each one by deducing the missing word from the clues. The clues include (*a*) the content; (*b*) the last word of the first line, which will rhyme with the missing word; and (*c*) the first letter and the number of letters given for the missing word.

> *Example:*
>
> When the butcher does use it, the cow is a griever,
>
> It's a sharp, axlike knife widely known as a c _ _ _ _ _ _ .

(The missing word, of course, is *cleaver*. It is defined in the couplet and rhymes with the word *griever*.)

Here are five for you:

1. With four legs and a tail and a yelp that's benign,

    You all know him, of course, as the family c _ _ _ _ _ _ .

2. He clowns on the stage in a limelight lagoon,

    Thriving only on laughter—a witless b _ _ _ _ _ _ _ .

3. It's odd and amusing, laughter its toll;

    It's whimsical, funny—in short, it is d _ _ _ _ _ .

4. You will gesture and grimace, yourself on parade,

    But no word do you speak as you play a c _ _ _ _ _ _ _ .

5. You burn to make money (defying your parson!);

    You burn for a profit. Now, Mister, that's a _ _ _ _ _ _ !

II. Now continue the same procedure with this quartet of quatrains, but here you must insert two words that rhyme with each other.

1. When the audience roars its approval,

    It's clear that the play is a h _ _ _ .
   But when it is short, fast, and funny,

    It's not really a play—it's a s _ _ _ _ .

2. Subside, subdue, subordinate

    (Just break the words a _ _ _ _ _ _ _).
   Submit, sub rosa, or subvert,

    Still S—U—B spells u _ _ _ _ _ !

These two are companion stanzas:

3. "Bring me soup, bisque, and chowder,

    Then roast pork and roast m_____,
Chocolate cake, pie, and ice cream,"

    Said the ravenous g_____.

4. "*I*'ll take only the best bit

    Of your salmon s_____,
But that bit must be super!"

    Warned the jaded g_____.

III. Finally there is a trio of limericks. Note that the first, second, and fifth lines share one rhyme, while the third and fourth lines have a different rhyme. Clues include (*a*) the content; (*b*) the number of letters in each missing word; (*c*) the first letter of each missing word; and (*d*) the definitions.

    There once was a captain i_____ (*angry*)
    Who wanted to chastise his mate.

       He stopped at an i_____ (*arm of the sea*)
       And dropped the mate *in* it,

    Then said, "Let him now be a s_____ !" (*small body of water connecting two larger bodies*)

    There once was a chauvinist male

    Who claimed that all women are f_____ (*delicate*),

       But his mind he did c_____ (*alter*)
       When he spied the huge range
    His wife carried home from a sale!

    There once was a burglar so d_____ (*dull, thick*)
    He left all the bills and stole cents.
       No wonder his teacher,
       His parents, and preacher

    All said that he needed some s_____ ! (*intelligence; judgment*)

IV. To Test Your Deductive Powers

    Refer to the text when necessary.

    1. How many lines are there in a couplet?   _____

                                    in a quatrain?   _____

    2. How many items are there in a quartet?   _____

3. Name three synonyms (words that have the same meaning) for "droll." _ _ _ _ _ _ _ _ _ _ _

_ _

4. From the context, can you guess what kind of gourmet is *jaded* (II, 4)? _ _ _ _ _ _ _ _ _ _ _

_ _ _ _ _ _ _ _ _ _ _ _ _ _ _ _ _ _

5. From the context, can you guess the meaning of *infectious* (second paragraph)?

_ _

V. Activity

Try writing one couplet,
            one quatrain,
            one limerick.

It really isn't difficult, and it can be fun. The quatrain is probably the easiest. Hint:
Make up a first line; then let your imagination help you to develop the rest of the "poem."

5
Catastrophe With a Banana Peel

As the foot can slip on a banana peel, so the tongue can slip on a word. The result can be embarrassment, financial loss, or—if you're lucky—just a chuckle. If you're unlucky, it can be a catastrophe (a great disaster)!

Here's a barrage (heavy artillery fire) of slips that should titillate your sense of humor.

I. Irish Bulls

These are as old as mankind and even harder to define. An Irish bull, said the poet Louis Untermeyer, is "an idea that starts out reasonably and ends ridiculously." It should sound sensible, even profound—until you think about it and realize that it's really absurd!

The best Irish bulls came into existence by accident. Can't you just hear an irate mother saying to her teenage son: "Why didn't you wake me up when you came in last night? You know I can't sleep until you're home!" It sounds right and natural until the ludicrous contradiction hits you. As a matter of fact, *you* have probably said, after falling asleep on the floor, "Why didn't you wake me up so I could go to sleep?"

Here are five more Irish bulls. In each case, see if you can spot the contradiction and explain the absurdity.

1. He told us that it was hereditary in his family to have no children. _____
   _____
   _____

2. I'd rather die than allow my body to be cremated! _____
   _____
   _____

3. Unfortunately, the status quo is always changing. _____
   _____
   _____

4. "Why, Mr. Speaker, honorable members never come down to this House without expecting to find their mangled remains lying on the table." (John Dillon in

   Parliament, 1882) _____
   _____
   _____

5. It is so hot in southern California that most of the inhabitants live somewhere else.
   _____
   _____

II. Boners

Boners are verbal blunders. They may occur because we misheard something (like the child who sang "London britches falling down") or because we do not understand the meaning of a word we want to use (like the young reporter who wrote that the "honeymooners were enjoying martial life"!) (You realize, of course, that he meant *marital* life, meaning "married life," and that *martial* means "warlike.")

Below are 10 boners. In each sentence spot the word that is misused and correct it.

1. The government of England is a limited mockery. _____

    _____

2. The French Revolution was fought for Liberty, Equality, and Paternity. _____

    _____

3. I wish I could vote, but I'm not legible. _____

    _____

4. The monastery unit of France is the franc. _____

    _____

5. The equator is a menagerie lion that runs around the middle of the earth. (Two boners

    in this sentence!) _____

    _____

6. As his hair began to secede, he considered getting a soufflé. (Two boners.) _____

    _____

7. The judge warned the witness not to purge himself. _____

    _____

8. A bigot is a man who has two wives. _____

    _____

9. All of the characters and plots in Mark Twain's stories are infectious. _____

    _____

10. After he swallowed the poison, he begged for an anecdote. _____

    _____

III. Spoonerisms

Well over a half century ago, the Reverend William A. Spooner, warden of New College, Oxford, was plagued by a tongue that slipped at all the wrong times. Once when he was sternly reprimanding a student, he said: "You have deliberately tasted two worms; you can leave Oxford by the town drain." What he meant, of course, was that the student had *wasted* two *terms* and should leave by the *down* train! It just came out a bit twisted. At another time the Reverend suggested to a bashful young husband that it is "kistomary to cuss the bride."

By now you probably realize that a spoonerism results when the initial sounds of two words are transposed (or reversed). See if you can disentangle the following spoonerisms by restoring the initial sounds to their proper positions.

1. Let me sew you to your sheet. _____

   _____

2. On the first of the month please kill me for my new bar. _____

   _____

3. As the police intensified the interrogation, the clam manned up. _____

   _____

4. In the 19th century, authors sometimes described Victoria as their "queer old dean."

   _____

5. With his powerful left fist he gave me a blushing crow. _____

   _____

IV. Typos

Typographical errors just happen. Occasionally they are quite amusing. Here is a menu that, by blending typos and spoonerisms, promises more amusement than gustatory (pertaining to taste) satisfaction. On the blank lines, mend it so that it will send the reader to dinner rather than to delirium!

Barely Soup

Chalk Pops With Rushmooms

Fired Potatoes

Bitter Beans

Chocolate Mouse or Pecan Lie

Toffee, Me, or Kilk

_____

_____

_____

_____

_____

_____

6
Sights and Sounds

There is more to a word than its meaning.

I. **A.** There's SIGHT. Look at

SQuabble	SQuawk
SQuall	SQueal
SQuander	SQuelch
SQuash	SQuiggle
SQuat	SQuirm

Are SQ words restful or restless? _ _ _ _ _ _ _ _ _ _ _ _ _ _ _ _ _

. . . moving or still? _ _ _ _ _ _ _ _ _ _ _ _

. . . pleasant or disagreeable? _ _ _ _ _ _ _ _ _ _ _ _ _ _ _ _ _ _ _

B. There's SOUND. Pronounce the same ten SQ words out loud. Which letters carry the strongest sound? _ _ _ _ _ _ _ _ _ _ _ _ _ _ What kind of sound is it? _ What do you do with your lips and tongue while you are making this sound? _

C. There's MEANING. Match the SQ words in the first column with their definitions in the second column.

_ _ _ _ 1. squall   *a.* to beat to a pulp; to crush

_ _ _ _ 2. squander   *b.* to quarrel; to bicker

_ _ _ _ 3. squash   *c.* to suppress; to silence

_ _ _ _ 4. squawk   *d.* to blow strongly for a short time

_ _ _ _ 5. squat   *e.* to look with eyes partly closed

_ _ _ _ 6. squeal   *f.* to spend extravagantly

_ _ _ _ 7. squirm   *g.* to utter a prolonged, shrill cry

_ _ _ _ 8. squelch   *h.* to twist about like a snake

_ _ _ _ 9. squabble   *i.* to sit on one's heels

_ _ _ 10. squint   *j.* to utter a harsh, abrupt scream

D. Write a paragraph of about 30 to 50 words describing the way *you* feel about SQ words. In the paragraph use as many SQ words as you can and be as humorous as possible.

_ _

Now analyze your paragraph.

1. Look at it. Does it *look* funny? _ _ _ _ _

2. Read it to a friend. Does it *sound* funny? _ _ _ _ _

3. To what extent do the appearance and sound of SQ contribute to the overall

   humorous effect? _

   _

II. The truth is that we do not know very much about the way the SIGHT and SOUND of words affect us . . . but we're quite certain that they do. There's something really amusing about

SQUIGGLE

while there's nothing amusing about

REMORSE.

Becoming sensitive to the SIGHT and SOUND of words will help you to tell jokes more effectively.

Try this quiz. There are no correct answers, but in choosing your answers and in comparing them with the answers of others, you will learn something about words and word-users.

Which word in the English language is

1. the funniest? _

2. the most beautiful? _

3. the saddest? _

4. the most frightening? _

5. the most boring? _

6. the ugliest? _

7. the most appetizing? _

8. the most sleep-inducing? _ _ _ _ _ _ _ _ _ _ _ _ _ _ _ _ _ _ _

III. **A Potpourri** (a mixture; a combination)

1. Is there a difference in the effect of the appearance of

WOW!   and   *wow!*

- -

- -

2. What difference is there in the SIGHT and SOUND of

WOW!   and   POW!

- -

- -

3. If you were telling a funny story, would you say a worm

meandered down your back?
or
squiggled down your back?

- - - - - - - - - - - - - - - - Why? -

- -

4. Which is round? Which is square?

A. - - - - - - - - - - -   B. - - - - - - - - - - -

A, of course, is square, and *B* is round. Does ☐ look like SQUARE? Does ☐ sound like SQUARE? Does ◯ look like ROUND? Does ◯ sound like ROUND?

Now here's a puzzle for you: Which came first, the word SQUARE or the figure ☐; the word ROUND or the figure ◯ ? If ☐ were called ROUND and ◯ were called SQUARE, would your attitudes toward ☐ or ◯ change? Does the "thing" affect its name, or does the name affect the "thing"?

Oh, well—square off for the next round!

7
Comic-Strip Mysteries

"Humor can be dissected, as a frog can, but the thing dies in the process and the innards are discouraging to any but the pure scientific mind." (E. B. White)

With that warning, proceed with dissection!

I.

BONER'S ARK

© King Features Syndicate 1972

1. What part does the *incongruous* play in this strip? _____
   _____

2. On what kind of wordplay does this joke depend? _____
   _____

3. Why is this comic strip called *Boner's Ark*? _____
   _____
   _____

Croker

by Brian Pickering

1. Describe briefly what you *see* in the first third of this strip. ------------------
   ----
   ----

2. How does the last word in the strip turn the speech into a joke? ------------------
   ----
   ----

3. Why was this comic strip printed in the *New York Teacher* newspaper? ------------
   ----

III.

FIGMENTS

By Dale Hale

DADDY WILL BE OUT JUST AS SOON AS HE PUNCHES THE CLOCK!

EMPLOYEE PARKING

DALE HALE

A FIGMENT OF
N. JENNINGS
S. F'DALE, NEW YORK

1. How does the "balloon" at the right differ from the "balloon" at the left? Why is it different? --

----

----

2. On what kind of wordplay does this joke depend? -----------------------------

----

----

3. Why is this comic strip called *Figments*? -----------------------------------

----

Four. The Mass Media, in So Many Words

1

Media Mania

Do you have the media mania? If you are an American living in the second half of the 20th century, you probably do.

Consider your day.

You are jarred into consciousness in the morning by the radio.

At school you are interrupted from time to time by announcements that come blaring over the public address system.

In social studies class, the Civil War is re-enacted on 16-mm. film, just for you.

In English class, a 35-mm. filmstrip tells all there is to know about Ernest Hemingway in barely 20 minutes.

At three o'clock, you and your friends go home, turn on your record players, and immerse yourselves in a sea of rock music.

After dinner is TV time, and along with millions of other Americans you laugh and cry and get angry, on cue, with the top 10 Nielsen-rated shows. Fortunately there are a few commercials: a chance to skim the daily newspaper or thumb through a magazine.

As you get ready for bed, you are surrounded by photographs—of friends, of movie stars, of athletes, of rock singers.

At last you turn in, and the radio that woke you up now lulls you back to sleep.

End of story.

*   *   *

What is this thing called *mass media* that has revolutionized our lives?

It began with the word *medium*, meaning simply a channel, or agency, of communication. Since there is more than one medium, the plural form, *media*, quickly came into use.

But the new media were aimed not at one person or a few but at many—at the masses. Hence, *mass media*.

I. The MASS MEDIA are hereby brought to trial. Below are the accusations most often made against some of the media. Read each accusation. Then state whether you agree or disagree with it, and why. (The key word or words in each charge are italicized. Be sure you understand them, even if it means consulting a dictionary.)

Charge 1: Television commercials *exploit* people's fears and children's desires.

Charge 2: All of the mass media are marked by a *lack of interaction* resulting in increased *passivity*.

- -

- -

Charge 3: Because of lack of *feedback*, the gap is growing wider between those who control the media and the masses who listen and watch.

- -

- -

- -

- -

Charge 4: Violence is *contagious*, and, thanks to the mass media, we are now experiencing an *epidemic* of violence.

- -

- -

- -

Charge 5: Through the mass media modern *technology* is eliminating differences and turning us all into carbon copies of each other.

- -

- -

- -

Charge 6: Electronic *amplification* of sound is resulting in loss of sensitivity and loss of hearing.

- -

- -

- -

Charge 7: Because of the mass media, doers are being *transformed* into spectators. There is less *involvement* than ever before in sports, theater, music, and politics.

- -

- -

- -

Charge 8: *Impersonality* is a mark of the mass media. Speakers no longer view us as individuals but as a nameless group of 200 million numbers.

- -

- -

- -

- -

II. To Test Your Memory

Match the words in the first column with the definitions in the second.

_ _ _ _ 1. exploit   *a.* a state of inactivity, of nonparticipation

_ _ _ _ 2. interaction   *b.* the absence of human qualities

_ _ _ _ 3. passivity   *c.* the application of science for commercial purposes

_ _ _ _ 4. feedback   *d.* mutual action or influence

_ _ _ _ 5. contagious   *e.* changed to a great extent

_ _ _ _ 6. technology   *f.* to make use of unfairly for selfish reasons

_ _ _ _ 7. amplification   *g.* condition of being actively a part of something

_ _ _ _ 8. transformed   *h.* information about the responses of people to influences acting upon them

_ _ _ _ 9. involvement   *i.* the act of making louder or more powerful

_ _ _ _ 10. impersonality   *j.* catching; tending to spread from one to another

2
The Boob Tube

Call it the "boob tube," the "idiot box," or what you will, television (preferably in color) is still America's most loved form of entertainment. You can survive without knowing the difference between *essence* and *existence*, but you are lost if you can't distinguish between *revival* and *rerun*!

Here are a few exercises to make you a versatile (many-talented) and vigorous (energetic) viewer!

I. You have just been hired to edit a TV guide for your local newspaper. When a reporter hands you the evening's schedule, you notice a number of blanks where words are missing. Can you complete the guide by inserting in the blanks the appropriate words from the list below?

ad lib	extravaganza	reminiscent
adapted	narrates	satirical
anchorman	parody	soap opera
animated	pre-empts	variety show
documentary	premiere	versatile
episode	prime	

7:30—Channel 201. *Barefoot on 42nd Street.* This TV _____ (*first appearance*) of the well-known romantic comedy features Jenny Linden. Sid Baxter

_____ (*rewrote for a new medium*) the stage play for this 2-hour flick.

Channel 206. *Trapeze Thrills.* Jo-Jo Jones _____ (*provides a running commentary for*) a film about the third ring in a three-ring circus.

8:00—Channel 206. *Ironstones.* In this _____ (*incident; one of a series of events*), Con and Ron romp engagingly in a _____ (*work that mimics something and holds it up for ridicule*) of a Jim Wain western.

8:30—Channel 201. *Paul Revere's Ride.* A fine _____ (*factual presentation of historical, political, or social events*) about a man and his horse.

_____ (*takes the place of*) Bonanza.

Channel 206. *ZBC News* with _____ (*coordinator of a news broadcast*) Hank Longfellow.

9:00—Channel 201. *The Flying Pun.* _____ (*mocking; exposing to ridicule*) sketches and _____ (*spontaneous; unplanned*) interviews highlight this _____ (*unrelated acts, including songs, skits, dances, etc.*).

Channel 206. *Thrills and Heartbreaks.* Sentimental _____ (*melodramatic, tear-jerking drama*) with the _____ (*able to play many roles*) Tessie Tears playing the martyred wife.

9:30—Channel 201. *Emeralds for Esmeralda.* A Victor Vent _____ (*an elaborate, usually highly expensive entertainment*) that is _____

_____ (*tending to recall the past*) of the best of the 1940 musicals.

Channel 206. *Sell or Be Sold.* A whole hour of _____
(*consisting of nonliving figures that move in a lifelike manner*) commercials brought

to you in _____ (*best; most preferred*) time.

II. You are a ZBC executive and you would like to sign up Zelda Zuider Zee, the *top-grossing* star, for a weekly *variety show*. In a letter she has asked the following questions: Is ZBC really a good *network*? Which *sponsors* will *underwrite* the show? Will the contract include a *renewable option*? Will it be *telecast* during *prime time*? Will it be *live* or *taped*? How many *dramatic vignettes* does the producer expect to include in each show?

As a ZBC executive, write a reply to Zelda answering her questions. Be sure you understand the italicized words, and use all of them correctly in your letter. But remember—*you* are trying to sell *her* an idea. Be persuasive!

_____

_____

_____

_____

_____

_____

_____

_____

III. **To Test Your Deductive Powers**

Using 5 of the 17 terms given at the beginning of this chapter, try to complete each statement below logically.

1. If your are planning to attend a(n) _____ , you may want to invest in a new wardrobe in order not to be out of step with the many celebrities who will be present.

2. If you wish to produce a(n) _____ , you will need much money, a great number of performers, and plenty of bright lights, ornate costumes, and elaborate sets.

3. Hoping to bring about some much-needed reform in hospital care, Sue wrote humorous but _____ articles about the trials and tribulations of a neglected patient.

4. Jed is so _____ that he not only wrote the play and acted in it, but also planned the lighting, the sound effects, and the sets.

5. She was an odd person: although she was generally passive, her features became _____ _____ as soon as the curtain went up.

3 The Celluloid Myth

Time was when giants strode across the screen, and producers ruled like tyrants. Then television intervened. Crowded movie houses gave way to family dens, and an ever-changing series of TV entertainers replaced the golden stars of Hollywood. Without question, the old magic had gone. Yet somehow the celluloid myth remains.

Perhaps it remains precisely because it is a myth. Like the traditional myth, this 20th-century version offers what all of us crave: romance, danger, and physical violence. It lets us climb mountains, pilot jets, and travel by rickshaw or Roman chariot. And we do all of these things in comfort and with little cost . . . thanks to the celluloid myth.

I. Here is an excerpt (section, part) from a movie script. Read it. Then, using your deductive powers and some common sense, try to answer the questions that follow the script.

Soup to the Rescue

1. *Pan shot. Interior of a diner, showing door, tables and chairs, floor, and counter. The diner is almost empty. It is midnight. Behind the counter is Joe Doe. Joe is 19 years old, has short dark hair, and is wearing a white jacket. At the counter, on a stool, is Jane Mane. Jane is 18 years old, has long blonde hair, and is wearing blue denims and a red blouse with gold trim. They are talking.*

2. *Medium Shot.*

   Joe (*pleading*).
     Come on, Jane—have a doughnut. Please!
   Jane (*sullenly*):
     Don't want one. Not from you.
   Joe:
     Don't be like that, hon. I *had* to work tonight.
   Jane (*tossing her hair*):
     That's what *you* say!
   Joe (*pushing cup toward her*):
     Well—have some coffee anyway.
   Jane:
     The coffee's bitter!

3. *Long shot: Joe and Jane talk, their heads close together. Their words can't be heard, but music plays softly in the background.*

4. *Extreme long shot: Joe leaves counter, takes a bowl, and fills it. He returns to counter, carrying bowl, which he places before Jane. Both lean over it for a moment. Then Joe straightens up triumphantly.*

5. *Close-up:*
   Jane (*smiling and amused, whispers softly*):
     Oh, Joe!

6. *Extreme close-up: Bowl of alphabet soup. In middle of bowl, letters spell out*

I LOVE YOU

a. What is a *pan shot?* --

----

b. What is a *medium shot?* --

----

c. What is a *close-up?* --

----

d. What is a *long shot?* --

----

e. Why would a director choose a long shot for #3 in the script? ---------------------

----

f. Why would a director choose a close-up for #5 in the script? ----------------------

----

g. *Pan* comes from *panorama* or *panoramic.* With this in mind, would you expect

panorama to refer to a wide area or a narrow area? -------------------------------
To a survey of several centuries in history or to an in-depth study of one event?

II. You should also know something about the kinds of people involved in the making and the viewing of a film. Match the people in the two columns.

---- 1. ingenue   *a.* a young female star

---- 2. starlet   *b.* an actor or actress hired to play a small part, often in a crowd scene

---- 3. producer   *c.* one who views a film and then gives his opinions regarding its worth

---- 4. critic

---- 5. extra   *d.* an actress playing a young, innocent, rather naive girl

   e. one who finances and supervises the making of a film

III. **To Test Your Memory and Your Deductive Powers**

1. The age of an actor or actress would be most obvious in (*a*) a long shot   (*b*) a medium shot   (*c*) a close-up. ----

2. If you want to cover the progress of a horse and rider across a wide expanse of plains, you would probably --------------- them.

3. A person who reads a book and then gives his opinion regarding its worth is called a(n)

----

4. When two people really care for each other, a disagreement is usually followed by a(n)

    --------------------------- .

5. A written text of a screenplay or telecast, including dialog, kinds of camera shots, and

    brief descriptions of proposed action, is called a(n) ----------------- .

IV. Activity

Write a description of a character caught up in a particular kind of emotional excitement, e.g., anger, joy, or hate. Include in your description sentences that depict him as if he were seen in a long shot, a medium shot, and a close-up. Note how using different points of view can sharpen your description of a character.

4
Stop the Press!

Newspapers are versatile. Their primary function is to communicate news, of course, but they may also be used to start fires, to protect floors from wet feet, to train puppies, and to swat flies. Clippings from newspapers fill the *vertical files* in libraries, and old bound volumes form the heart of the newspaper *morgue*—a place where dead news is kept until some researcher chooses to resurrect it.

I. You probably know a good deal about newspapers already, but here is a quick review of the three kinds of items that can be found in any newspaper.

newsstory: an article that presents an impartial report of a recent event

editorial: an article that expresses the opinions of an editor or publisher

feature: an "extra"—article, column, or cartoon—meant to attract attention. Sometimes it deals with a trivial idea, handled lightly. Sometimes it deals with an important idea, which it examines from several angles. Sometimes it emphasizes the human-interest aspects of a situation.

Below are nine adjectives. Link each one with one kind of newspaper item. Use each only once.

argumentative	humorous	objective
concise	interpretative	persuasive
factual	intriguing	sensational

Newsstory	Editorial	Feature
1. _____	4. _____	7. _____
2. _____	5. _____	8. _____
3. _____	6. _____	9. _____

II. Here are a few more newspaper-related words you should know:

beat	obituary	syndicated
column	slanted	

Complete each of the following statements by inserting one of the above words or answering the question:

1. If, under his own by-line, a newspaper writer submits daily an article in which he gives his opinions about different topics, he writes a(n) _____ .

2. If this daily piece is printed in many newspapers, not just in one, it is said to be

_____ .

3. You know what a policeman's *beat* is; what is a reporter's *beat*? _____

_____

4. An article that is a biography of someone who has just died is called a(n) _____

_____ .

5. If a newsstory or a headline is intended to favor one side of a dispute or one person involved in it, that newsstory or headline is said to be _____ .

III. To Test Your Memory and Your Deductive Powers

1. The container in a library in which newspaper clippings are kept is called a(n) _____ .

2. A person who can dance and sing, who is skilled in photography, who writes well, and who runs a business efficiently and profitably might well be described as _____ .

3. The room in a newspaper building that houses bound copies of the paper, old photos, and other temporarily dead resources is known as the _____ .

4. You know what a *headline* is; what kind of person is a *headliner*? _____ _____

5. A reporter's name under a headline or title of a story he wrote is a(n) _____ _____ .

6. You know what an editorial is. If a reporter *editorializes* in a newsstory, what is he doing? _____ _____

7. You know now that a *feature* is designed to attract attention. What is meant when we say a grocery story manager has decided to *feature* a particular brand of coffee? _____ _____

You are a newspaper reporter. You hear about a four-alarm fire in the shopping plaza. You write three stories about the fire.

8. The first story you write is an angry article in which you try to persuade your readers to oust the local politicians who permitted the careless storage that led to the fire. This story is a(n) _____ .

9. The second story you write is a factual account, totally objective, of what actually happened at the scene of the fire. This story is a(n) _____ .

10. The third story you write is a half-amusing, half-tearful account of a five-year-old whose teddy bear has been burned. This story is a(n) _____ .

5
Air Waves

When in 1895 Guglielmo Marconi gave a demonstration of radiotelegraphy, he could hardly have realized what he was starting. He couldn't have foreseen the ship-to-shore communication that developed before World War I, nor the aircraft-to-ground communication that developed during the war. Even less could he have foreseen the way the world was drenched in the sounds of radio during the 20's and 30's.

In the late 1940's when television made its debut (official beginning), it seemed that radio might be dead. It did stagger for a bit but then bounced back stronger than ever. Today it is the rare American home that doesn't have more than one radio: one to wake people up and give forth the daily news; one in each car to provide companionship to lone drivers; one in the kitchen to offer a background of music and news for the cook and dishwasher; and often several small transistor radios to "travel." It is no longer strange—as Ray Bradbury, the science-fiction writer noted in horror—to see a couple walking down the street, each in a self-imposed isolation created by a small radio held to the ear.

For good or for evil, radio is with us. We can use it or abuse it. Since this is so, we must know a little about it.

I. Radio is a *sound* instrument. It appeals solely to the ear. One receives information from it *aurally*—through the ear. Therefore, it becomes important to be aware of *voices*. Below are 10 adjectives that describe different kinds of voices. Can you match the adjectives with their definitions?

    ---- 1. nasal   *a.* scornful; ridiculing

    ---- 2. affected   *b.* jolly; merry

    ---- 3. caressing   *c.* ringing; echoing

    ---- 4. strident   *d.* affectionate; kindly

    ---- 5. mocking   *e.* not capable of being heard

    ---- 6. inaudible   *f.* projected, at least partly, through the nose

    ---- 7. resonant   *g.* gloomy; funereal

    ---- 8. vibrant   *h.* not natural; artificial

    ---- 9. jovial   *i.* grating; shrill

    ---- 10. sepulchral   *j.* pulsing with life

II. In addition to kinds of voices, there are different ways of expressing oneself. Can you match these?

    ---- 1. to mutter   *a.* to cry with a low, whining sound

    ---- 2. to croon   *b.* to laugh softly, as if to oneself

    ---- 3. to chuckle   *c.* to hum or sing in a low, soft voice

    ---- 4. to jabber   *d.* to speak complainingly in low, indistinct tones

    ---- 5. to whimper   *e.* to speak rapidly or indistinctly

III. Although radio is limited to sound, it can produce many different kinds of programs. All of the following are offered regularly by various radio stations. Match the program with its description.

concert   newscast   panel show
drama   opera   quiz show
farce   operetta   serial
melodrama

1. A drama or comedy presented in daily or weekly installments is called a(n) _____ .

2. A prose or verse work performed by actors is called a(n) _____ .

3. A dramatic presentation with a great deal of suspense, and sensational episodes, is called a(n) _____ .

4. A drama set to music is called a(n) _____ .

5. A musical presentation that is light both in content and style and that often includes spoken dialogue is a(n) _____ .

6. A musical performance by vocalists or instrumentalists is called a(n) _____ .

7. A question-and-answer show, with prizes going to the winners, is called a(n) _____ .

8. A group of people discussing an issue or answering questions is known as a(n) _____ .

9. A spoken report of events in the news is called a(n) _____ .

10. A play filled with improbable but humorous happenings is known as a(n) _____ .

IV. Following are bits of dialogue from radio scripts. You should be able to detect the speaker's mood from the words alone. Can you? One is *arrogant*, one is *belligerent*, one is *derisive*, one is *incoherent*, and one is *ruthless*. Which is which?

1. "I mean—that is to say—well, you know how it is— if everyone—I mean—if everyone continues—well, you know!"

    1. _____

2. "You, my dear boy, are hardly capable of speaking about *family*. Now my people came over on the *Mayflower*. We know this country, and it is ours!"

    2. _____

3. "If 10 people must be destroyed to assure my comfort, so be it."

    3. _____

4. "Go ahead! Just say it! And if you do, so help me, I'll punch you in the jaw!"

4. _____

5. "So you're going to climb to the top of Three-Mile Mountain by yourself, are you? You who stagger and stumble on an ordinary stairway? *That* I've got to see!"

5. _____

V. A Catechism (question-and-answer collection) on Radio

1. Which of the following shows could *not* be presented on radio? (*a*) concert   (*b*) pantomime   (*c*) drama

1. ____

2. Which of the following murderers would be most effective in a radio mystery?   (*a*) one who leaves a large "X" on the door   (*b*) one who wears a stocking mask   (*c*) one who whistles a particular tune

2. ____

3. Which of the following directions would you, a radio director, give to an actor?   (*a*) Breathe audibly.   (*b*) Blink your eyes.   (*c*) Smile broadly.

3. ____

4. What is the difference between *monaural* sound and *binaural* sound? (Keep in mind the meanings of the prefixes.) _____

_____

_____

5. List *five* situations in which radio is a highly useful medium:

_____

_____

_____

_____

_____

VI. Activity

Write a brief radio script (about 200 words). Then go through the script, and insert directions for each segment of dialogue so that the actors will know how to read the lines.

6
Say Cheese!

How do you take a home movie? Or 35-mm. slides? Or just snapshots?

You put film in a camera and shoot. Right?

Wrong!

Taking pictures requires skill, the same kind of skill required in writing an essay or preparing a speech.

I. A. First start with an idea or topic. (You might, for example, wish to take pictures of your brother Jim and his graduation from high school.)

Second, find an angle. (One possibility: This is the day when Jim becomes an adult.)

Third, plan the *sequence* of your shots. For example:

1. You might begin with a picture of your brother several days before graduation. He is studying for a final exam. He is tired and discouraged.

2. The next shot might show him looking at a list of seniors who have "made it." This time he is laughing.

3. The third shot might catch him as he helps plan his graduation party.

Now *you* supply suggested shots #4–9 that will lead logically to #10.

4. _____
_____

5. _____
_____

6. _____
_____

7. _____
_____

8. _____
_____

9. _____
_____

10. The last shot will be a close-up showing the cap and gown packed in a box to be returned. Next to it lies a notice from the army or a letter from the college he plans to attend—an end and a beginning.

B. You now have a script—but it is not yet complete. Go back and note next to each shot whether it should be a long shot (from a distance, including several people or objects), a medium shot (one or two people, with the whole body shown), or a close-up (usually only one person, and just the face). Remember that a long shot allows *perspective* (placement of people to give a feeling of depth and to suggest their relationship), while a close-up is more *intimate* (close and personal). #1 would be good as a medium shot, while #2 might demand an extreme long shot showing a group of seniors craning their necks as they try to check the graduating list. Note also whether each shot should be *horizontal* (wider than tall) or *vertical* (taller than wide).

C. Next, jot down next to each shot the probable setting: e.g., #1—Jim at his desk in his bedroom; #2—Jim standing in the school corridor with six other students; etc. Vary backgrounds when possible. When you have finished, you will have a *shooting script*.

D. If you plan to provide either music or narration, you will have to be concerned with *synchronization*—precise timing so the sound will exactly match the movement and sequence of the pictures.

II. Here is some additional information. Read carefully.

1. You *focus* on a subject in order to get a clear image.

2. To achieve an *illusion* of motion, have your subject assume a walking position.

3. To suggest Jim's hopes of graduating, you can take a picture of him studying, and then *superimpose* upon it a blurred, faint picture of a cap and gown.

4. Be conscious of the *composition* of your pictures: a doorway can frame a person; the branch of a tree can frame a bird.

5. When shooting, avoid *overexposure* (too much light) as well as *underexposure* (too little light).

III. To Test Your Memory and Your Deductive Powers

Each of the following sentences can be completed by inserting a photography-related word from this chapter. However, these sentences are not about photography. You must, therefore, remember the photographic meaning of the word and then apply that meaning to a different situation. Can you do it?

1. Since we must arrive at exactly the same moment, let us _____ our watches.

2. When one lies on a studio couch, one is in a _____ position; when one stands erect, one is in a _____ position.

3. _____ to the rays of the sun can cause severe burns and even cancer of the skin.

4. If you are having trouble with math, learn to _____ on one type of problem before tackling more difficult kinds.

5. When an artist places a dark tree in the upper right-hand corner of his canvas and a small, dark stream in the lower left-hand corner, he is paying attention to

   _____ .

6. If you want to have the _____ that you are seven feet tall, walk on stilts!

7. When putting together a complicated toy or appliance, you should not work haphazardly but follow the instructions in order, that is, in _____ .

8. Your relationships with your classmates are not usually as _____ as your relationships with members of your family.

7

It's Free!

It's free, isn't it? No strings attached! No obligation! Buy now, pay in 6 months—or 6 years—or 60 years! Who cares? It's free!

But is it?

Can you match the free "things" in the first column with their definitions in the second?

I.   ____ 1. throwaway

   ____ 2. giveaway

   ____ 3. brochure

   ____ 4. advertisement

   ____ 5. junk mail

   ____ 6. insert

   ____ 7. sample

   ____ 8. demonstration

a. a notice meant to attract public attention

b. a representative piece; a part of a whole

c. a handbill or circular that is often discarded after being accepted

d. mail that is not solicited and that is often "filed" in the wastebasket

e. something given away free

f. the act of showing how a product works

g. a pamphlet; a booklet

h. a circular separately printed and inserted in a newspaper

The above are all forms of advertising. They work, of course—at least part of the time. If they did not, they wouldn't continue to be used. Of what value are they? It depends. A demonstration may be honest and informative, or it may be misleading. Circulars may be a pain-in-the-neck, but they may also be helpful in determining a week's menu and in ascertaining which products are most favorably priced in which stores.

So it depends—on what is said and on how it is said.

II. Here are a few techniques often used in modern advertising. Becoming aware of them will help you to become a sharper reader and a more discerning consumer.

1. *gimmick:* a tactic or device meant to promote a project; e.g., a raffle, a contest, or a prize in a package of cereal

2. *slogan:* a catch phrase used to promote a product; e.g., "If it's _____, it's got to be good!"

3. *fine print:* the very small print that modifies and makes an offer less attractive. Many advertisers apparently hope no one will read it.

4. *flattery:* a phrase or statement that makes the reader feel special—distinguished in some way. Through this device the advertiser tries to create a favorable attitude toward his product.

5. *non sequitur:* a conclusion that does not follow from the previous statement. "I watch baseball on TV just as you do. Vote for me—I'll be the kind of mayor you want!" (His watching baseball on TV has nothing to do with the kind of mayor he will be—or with the kind you want.)

III. Read the following advertisement carefully:

COME ONE, COME ALL!

In honor of the glorious Fourth, we at Boom Town are making this one-time offer to our favorite customers! Not only do we have the brightest rockets and the loudest firecrackers in town, we also have beautiful, shiny, sleek motorbikes—and *they're free*!* Yes, that's what we said—free! Imagine riding down the pike on your very own bike!

Can you *afford* to go anywhere else for this year's fireworks? With an offer like this, you *know* that only at Boom Town will you get the wildest pyrotechnic display in the whole U.S.A.!

Remember—it's Boom Town for a Booming Fourth! Don't *you* want to be a good American?

*Two motorbikes will be given absolutely free to the first two customers who buy at least $20,000 worth of our merchandise.

Now select from the above advertisement a word, phrase, or sentence that illustrates each of the five most common promotional techniques.

1. *gimmick:* _____

_____

2. *slogan:* _____

3. *fine print:* _____

_____

4. *flattery:* _____

5. *non sequitur:* _____

_____

_____

IV. Where do *you* rate on the "awareness index"? Try this quiz and find out. After each of the statements below, explain briefly the trick, half-truth, or misleading phrase used. Then check the score at the end to see where you stand on the "awareness index"!

1. Boom Town tries harder. We've got to be good!

_____

_____

2. Thomas Jefferson bought our firecrackers. So did Abraham Lincoln. They knew quality when they saw it. Do you?

_____

_____

3. Think of it, kids! Fifty giant firecrackers packed in a bright red firetruck! This is for you! Ask Dad to get you the whole shebang! Only $1 each. (Firetruck is extra.)

----

4. Our company was founded in 1776—the same year our country was founded. For the most American fireworks ever, buy at Boom Town.

----

5. Santa Claus in July! Where? Where else? Boom Town, of course! Santa will be here with his eight shiny reindeer—an out-of-season visit for Boom Town's favorite customers! Won't your kids love it when Santa personally hands each of them the fireworks you've chosen? When you really love them, you want to give them joy all year round. At least that's how we feel . . . .

Score: If you were able to detect the misleading tactic in all five, you may apply now—for a job as an ad writer or as a detective first grade!

If you spotted three or four of the misleading tactics, you're doing all right. You're up there with most of us.

If you spotted only two of the misleading tactics, you're a trifle gullible, and you should let a friend hold your wallet whenever you go shopping!

If you scored one or zero, you should reserve a ticket for the first passenger rocket to the moon. You're too trusting for this paradise of piracy that we call Earth!

8
Political Arena

Fill in the blanks:

Your name is _____ . You
are running for the position of _____ (school
trustee, village trustee, mayor, or other). You are officially registered as a
_____ (Democrat, Republican, other).

I. Before you can begin your campaign, there are a few things you should know. You will need a *campaign manager*: someone who will set up speaking engagements, supervise the printing of brochures, provide bumper stickers, etc. And you will need a *platform*: the principles or ideas that a party or candidate supports.

According to most experienced politicians, you should concentrate on one or two major changes rather than treat superficially a dozen or more. Take a minute and choose one *plank* for your *platform*.

_____

_____

II. Now there are many methods by which you can take your plank to the people.

First, you can provide bumper stickers. Your slogan should be short, memorable, and meaningful. Here are a few from past presidential campaigns:

A FULL DINNER PAIL   (McKinley)

KEEP COOL WITH COOLIDGE   (Coolidge)

I LIKE IKE   (Eisenhower)

ALL THE WAY WITH LBJ   (Johnson)

Make up a good slogan that could be printed on bumper stickers for *your* campaign.

```
┌──────────────────────────────────────────────────┐
│                                                    │
└──────────────────────────────────────────────────┘
```

Second, you can distribute circulars or brochures. Political reality demands that you do *not* be modest. Don't be afraid to use *superlatives* (finest, best, most brilliant, etc.). Complete the circular on the next page.

```
┌─────────────────────────────────────────────────────────┐
│                        V O T E                          │
│         for  _____            │
│                        (name)                           │
│         for  _____ .          │
│                        (office)                         │
│       _____ is the _____ person for     │
│       (He, She)       (one or more words)               │
│    this job. _____ is exceeded│
│            (His, Her)                                   │
│         only by _____ .       │
│                (his, her)                               │
│       VOTE for  _____ !       │
└─────────────────────────────────────────────────────────┘
```

III. Here are a few qualities that a *good* politician should have:

initiative—the ability to form and introduce a new idea or plan

integrity—total loyalty to one's principles of behavior

conviction—a strong and firm belief

commitment—a state of being strongly bound to some course of action

diplomacy—the use of tact in dealing with people

Your local newspaper has asked your campaign manager for a paragraph or two describing you, the candidate, and your platform. Be a "ghost"* for your campaign manager, and write the article yourself. Use all five of the above terms.

IV. Since you are running for office, you are undoubtedly familiar with all of the common terms related to presidential politics. For example, you *do* know all of these terms, don't you?

*ghost—one who writes and gives credit for authorship to another individual

caucus   incumbent
concedes   lame duck
dark horse   lobbyist
favorite son   primaries
inauguration   projected winner

Now prove you know them by inserting the correct word or words from the above list in each of the blanks below.

1. A(n) _____ President has a head start toward re-election. After all, he is already page-one news.

2. Jim Baker may have no political office, but as a(n) _____, he tries to promote some legislation and to block other legislation.

3. No one had ever seriously considered that Congressman as a Presidential candidate.

    He was a real _____.

4. Often a state, conscious of the pride of its citizens, casts its first ballot for a(n) _____

    _____.

5. At 10 P.M., before the polls had closed in the Western states, several TV stations

    announced the _____.

6. If one candidate is receiving most of the votes, the losing candidate usually _____

    _____ the election.

7. Many states hold _____ to determine who the most effective candidate would be for a particular party.

8. During a convention, state delegates often _____ to try to come to a unanimous or nearly unanimous decision.

9. In the weeks between the election of a new President and the date he takes office, the

    outgoing President is known as a(n) _____ President.

10. At the _____ the successful candidate takes the oath of office and officially begins his term.

V. Activity

    Plan a class discussion on one or more of the following questions:

1. What kind of impact does a "spot" announcement on radio or television carry? Can you give two psychological reasons for its growing popularity?
2. What kind of political candidate is most telegenic? Is being telegenic likely to affect an election? Should it?
3. Which aspects of TV coverage emphasize a candidate's ideas? Which emphasize a candidate's personality? What is meant by a candidate's *image*?
4. Do computer predictions affect final results? Are they helpful or harmful?
5. Are the mass media a major factor in determining the outcomes of modern elections? Exactly how and why? What is the significance of your answer?

9
Media Mysteries

1. Joe Blow has been accused of stealing a car at 9:35 P.M. on Tuesday. He insists he is innocent. "I couldn't have stolen the car at 9:35," he told the police. "Every Tuesday night I give a cooking lesson on TV from 9 to 10 P.M. How could I be at the TV station and at the scene of the crime simultaneously?"

   Joe Blow *was* guilty. Why might his alibi not really be an alibi at all?

   ----

2. When Charlie Snow arrived home, his wife turned off the television set and clobbered him with a mixing bowl. All injured innocence, Charlie promptly took his wife to court.

   "Your Honor, I was working. That's why I was late. I was working hard to earn money for *her!*"

   "You're lying, Charlie Snow," his wife Adelaide said calmly. "You were having a real wild time at the fights. That's what you were doing!"

   Adelaide had been in the house all day and had had no visitors or telephone calls. Yet she was right—Charlie was lying. How could she have learned that he was at the fights?

   ----

3. Tracy's campaign manager, Ray Gray, came up with this sparkling slogan for his candidate:

   ### TRACY FOR TRUSTEE—TRUST HIS TEMERITY!

   Tracy lost the election. When he finally realized why, he fired Gray. What did he find out?

   ----

4. Five witnesses were called by the prosecution. Each claimed to be an expert in one of the media. After hearing their testimony regarding their credentials (evidence regarding their qualifications), the judge ruled that three of them were not qualified. Which three were not qualified? How did the judge know they were not?

   a. The Director: I've never used a shooting script. You see, I've never directed a western.

b. *The Editor:* I write editorials. They reflect my own opinions, not necessarily those of our readers.

c. *The Cameraman:* I pan a lot—especially during a scene when I want to capture the tiniest change of expression on the face of the heroine.

d. *The Producer of Radio Programs:* I've been in this field a long time. I know how to select a nice strident voice for the part of a romantic young girl, or a sepulchral voice for a vigorous athlete. Voices are my business!

e. *The Photographer:* I want clear, well-planned pictures. Before I shoot, I think about composition and proper exposure. Photography is an art!

First nonexpert: _____

_____

_____

Second nonexpert: _____

_____

_____

Third nonexpert: _____

_____

_____

Five. Putting in a Good Word for Animals

1
Big-Game Hunting

One of the most popular vacations today is the *safari*—an exploring or hunting expedition in East Africa. Recently the mini-safari became possible as "safari-lands" opened up in several different parts of this country. For a modest fee, you drive—in your own car—through a man-made wilderness. Prides of lions cavort a few feet from your closed window, and curious giraffes nibble doubtfully on the roof of your car. Ostriches, panthers, elephants, and monkeys are all within sight, and often within reach. You are free to shoot as many animals as you like—as long as your weapon is a camera!

Since even a mini-safari demands some planning, however, proceed with this series of mini-lessons in *ethology*, the science that studies the normal behavior of animals.

I. Lesson One

The Latin word, *vorare*, means "to devour," "to eat greedily." With this in mind and with the help of the given clues, see if you can describe the general diet of the following types of animals.

a. *carnivorous* animals (clue: Remember chili con *carne*.) _

_ _

b. *herbivorous* animals (clue: You know what *herbs* are.) _

_ _

c. *omnivorous* animals (clue: Remember that *omni*potent means "*all*-powerful," and *omni*scient means "*all*-knowing.") _

_ _

II. Lesson Two

Mammal is a class of *vertebrate* animals—that is, animals having a backbone, or spinal column. There are more than 15,000 *species*, or different kinds, of mammals. The highest order of the mammal is the *primates*; primates include humans, apes, and monkeys.

Use the above four italicized words to complete this paragraph: A man and an

elephant are two different _ _ _ _ _ _ _ _ _ _ _ _ _ _ _ _ _ _ _ of animals. Since they both have

spinal columns, they are both _ _ _ _ _ _ _ _ _ _ _ _ _ _ _ _ _ _ _. Both are also _ _ _ _ _ _ _ _ _ _

_ _ _ _ _ _ _ _ _ _ _ . Man, however, is a _ _ _ _ _ _ _ _ _ _ _ _ _ _ _ _ _ _ _, while the elephant
is not.

III. Lesson Three

Just as we are interested in the behavior of humans, so we are also interested in the behavior of animals. Much animal behavior results from an innate (inborn) impulse, or demand. This is called *instinct*. Instinctive behavior has nothing to do with reason. Identify one kind of instinctive animal behavior. _ Now identify one kind of instinctive human behavior. _ Note that *instinct* is something that humans and animals share, although in animals it is much stronger and in humans it is frequently modified by reason.

Some animals are *gregarious:* they tend to travel in groups. Can you name two animals that are *gregarious*? _ _ _ _ _ _ _ _ _ _ _ _ _ _ _ _ and _ _ _ _ _ _ _ _ _ _ _ _ _ _ _ _. Are humans *gregarious*? _ _ _ _ _ _ Is there a difference between the *gregariousness* of animals and the *gregariousness* of humans? If so, describe the difference. _ _ _ _ _ _ _ _ _ _ _ _ _ _ _ _

_ _

Until recently, certain animals were considered *aggressive*—inclined to act boldly, often in hostile fashion. For centuries hunters have considered lions and bears *aggressive*. Now many ethologists claim that when *they* meet these animals in the wilderness, they do not find them aggressive. Can you suggest a reason why a particular animal may be aggressive toward a hunter but not toward an ethologist? _

_ _

Many animals are *predatory:* they hunt, catch, and eat other animals. The animal that is caught and eaten is called the *prey*. But *prey* can also be a verb: a fox *preys* on chickens. The chicken, therefore, is the *prey*. Make up a sentence containing these two very different words: *pray* and *prey*. _

_ _

IV. Lesson Four: Back to the Safari

During this safari you will meet six wild animals. Below is a cluster of four clues for each of the six animals. How many of them can you identify?

1. *a.* This mammal is omnivorous, as some visitors to Yellowstone National Park have sadly learned.
   b. Although apparently clumsy, it is really quite agile—it can climb trees and even dance.
   c. Two constellations have been named after it.
   d. It has a shaggy coat, a short tail, and "flat feet."

   It is a(n) _ _ _ _ _ _ _ _ _ _ _ _ _ _ _ _.

2. *a.* This mammal, although big enough to swallow a man, is herbivorous.
   b. It is gregarious and is reputed to have an excellent memory.
   c. It is a symbol for one of the major political parties in the United States.
   d. It has a thick, almost hairless skin and a long, flexible trunk.

   It is a(n) _ _ _ _ _ _ _ _ _ _ _ _ _ _ _ _.

3. *a.* This mammal, a feline, is carnivorous.
   b. It is a predatory animal and, when hungry, considers everything and everyone in the wilderness as fair prey.
   c. It is the national emblem of Great Britain.
   d. It has a tawny coat, and the male has a long, heavy mane.

   It is a(n) _____.

4. *a.* This large, powerful, and terrifying-looking mammal is actually herbivorous.
   b. It has quite a snout crowned with one or two horns.
   c. It is native to Africa and Asia.
   d. Its thick skin is its best-known characteristic, leading to the saying "You are as

   thick-skinned as a _____!"

   It is a(n) _____.

5. *a.* This fairly small mammal is carnivorous.
   b. It is predatory and has upright ears and a pointed snout.

   c. Its name is used as the first element in the words _____glove,

   _____hound,_____trot, and

   _____hole, and as the first word in the combination

   _____ terrier.
   d. Its long bushy tail is as well known as its sly, foxy nature.

   It is a(n) _____.

6. *a.* This mammal is a large primate.
   b. It is most at home in the forests of equatorial Africa.
   c. Its name is used as an epithet (descriptive term) for humans who act brutishly or rudely.
   d. It has a stocky body and coarse dark hair.

   It is a(n) _____.

V. **To Test Your Memory and Your Deductive Powers**

   1. Any animal that has a spinal column is properly called a(n) _____.

   2. A person who studies normal animal behavior is called a(n) _____.

   3. When a baby cries when he feels he is falling, his reaction is properly called a(n) _____

      _____.

   4. The word element *omni-* means _____.

   5. An *omnipotent* God is one who is _____.

   6. Humans are (carnivorous, herbivorous, omnivorous) _____.

7. A person who enjoys going to parties and participating in parades is probably _____
_____.

8. What is meant when someone says that remorse *preys* on his mind? _____
_____

9. What single characteristic related to bone structure is shared by all mammals? _____
_____

10. Instinct is *innate*; Plato said knowledge is *innate*. What does *innate* mean? _____
_____

2
The Zoo Story

Zoos are *not* as old as man—but they do have a long history. There is no way of knowing who dreamed up the first zoo or where it was located, but we do know that a fully developed zoo existed in China in 1100 B.C. under the emperor Wu Wang. It was called "Intelligence Park," reflecting the sophisticated educational goals of its founders. Today almost every large city has a zoo, and it is usually a very popular attraction on Sunday afternoons.

Animals do not generally have to be taken care of. In the wilderness or in the jungle, they are independent, making their own shelters, finding their own food, discovering companionship or comfort as required. But when animals are transported into an alien (foreign, strange) environment, the picture changes. They become totally dependent, and all kinds of people are needed to look after them.

I. Here are five kinds of "animal keepers." Match each with his job description.

---- 1. zoologist   *a.* one who prepares, stuffs, and mounts the skins of animals

---- 2. curator   *b.* one who feeds and takes daily care of the animals

---- 3. taxidermist*   *c.* one who specializes in the study of animals

---- 4. veterinarian   *d.* one who directs or manages a museum, zoo, or library

---- 5. keeper   *e.* one who is trained to treat ill or injured animals

II. Now let's try a few "zoo problems."

A. *First:* You're a keeper, new at the job, and you are trying to match five animals with their rations. Waiting to be fed are an *elephant*, a *koala* (the original teddy bear), a *python*, a *sea lion*, and a *walrus*. To which of the above would you give

   a. fresh eucalyptus leaves? ----------------

   b. soft-shelled clams? ----------------

   c. 200 pounds of hay, a dozen loaves of bread, and a huge salad? ----------------

   d. 8 to 10 pounds of fresh fish? ----------------

   e. a 40-pound pig (but only once in a while)? ----------------

B. *Second:* This time your problem is to match five animals with five behavior patterns. The animals include a *kangaroo*, a *giraffe*, a *porcupine*, a *skunk*, and a *porpoise*. Which of them belongs with each behavior pattern described below? (You may wish to consult a dictionary.)

   a. This mammal, when frightened, emits a malodorous secretion. ----------------

   b. This mammal, when frightened, "shoots" quills into its opponent's flesh. --------
   ----

*The taxidermist, of course, looks after animals in a rather special way!

c. This mammal, like all marsupials, carries its young in an abdominal pouch. _____

_____

d. This aquatic mammal has a high intelligence, likes to gambol with humans, and is reported to have saved people from drowning. _____

e. This ruminant mammal uses its long neck to reach the delicate leaves it prefers for its lunch. _____

C. *Third:* Working around animals, you develop an interest in slang expressions based on animal traits or actions. How would you explain the italicized terms in the sentences below to someone who doesn't know much about animals?

a. Graft? Of course. Didn't you know he wants to *feather his own nest*? _____

_____

_____

b. They weren't doing anything—just *monkeying around*. _____

_____

c. Talk about equality if you like, but I'm the strongest and I want the *lion's share*!

_____

_____

d. The *wildcat strike* disrupted all transportation and all business in a 5-mile area.

_____

_____

e. Last week the stock market was *bearish*; today it's *bullish*. I guess I'll buy. _____

_____

_____

III. **To Test Your Memory and Your Deductive Powers**

1. If a person is an *alien* in the United States, was he born in this country? _____

2. The director of a museum is called a _____.

3. The original teddy bear was a _____.

4. A *python* is a large, nonvenomous _____.

5. *Malodorous* means _____.

6. Obviously, then, the word element "mal" means _____. Therefore, *maladjusted* means _____.

7. An aquatic mammal is one that spends all or much of its time in the _____.

8. Animals that carry their young in abdominal pouches are called _ _ _ _ _ _ _ _ _ _ _ _ _ _ _ _ _ _.

9. Is a mammal that has a four-section stomach and that chews its cud called a marsupial or a ruminant? _

10. If you wish to have the head of a moose mounted for the wall of your den, what kind of specialist would you call? _

3
With Rod and Reel

"Or would you rather be a *fish*?"

Several decades ago, when a popular song asked that question, few people took it seriously. Yet it is an intriguing idea. To a mammal, a fish is alien—*different*—more different, in some ways, than the Martian that is purely a creature of our imaginations.

Well, then, what exactly *is* a fish?

A fish is cold-blooded, while we are warm-blooded.

A fish is aquatic, while we are of the land.

A fish is a vertebrate; so are we.

A fish has no neck; we, of course, do.

A fish breathes through gills; we breathe with lungs.

A fish has fins (two pairs of appendages) that enable it to move and steer; we have arms and legs (two pairs of appendages) that enable us to move and manipulate.

A fish has a tail that propels it and scales that cover it; we do not.

No wonder a fish seems alien; it is!

Some "Believe-It-or-Not," Strictly True Fish Stories

The climbing perch of East India can run along the ground. It can even climb trees to a height of six or seven feet.

Flying fish can soar through the air for a quarter of a mile, their large pectoral (chest) fins supporting the body.

The tuna may weigh 1,000 pounds and may be 10 feet long.

The whale shark sometimes grows to a length of 65 feet!

I. Writing a Real Fish Story

If you have ever been fishing, you know how much fun it is to tell—after the event—a good fish story. It requires *hyperbole* (exaggeration) and a long string of colorful words.

Develop the second (and possibly the first) by completing the following statements. Each statement is followed by three words. Circle the one you would choose if you were telling a "fish story," and give the reason for each choice.

1. The sailfish I hooked was 30 inches long. It was _____. (miniscule, large, gargantuan) _____

   _____

2. Although I had all the advantages, it fought me for 30 minutes. It was indeed a _____ _____ fish. (craven, courageous, valiant) _____

   _____

3. Repeatedly, with the cruel hook dragging at its mouth, it turned for "one last" _____ _____ run for freedom. (feeble, hard, desperate) _____

   _____

4. But at last even its _____ heart succumbed. (flaccid, strong, stalwart) _____

_____

5. As it rose above the surface, the sun, dancing on the water-splashed scales, transformed the dying creature of the sea into a(n) _____ jewel. (pallid, variegated, iridescent) _____

6. For a moment, my own heart stopped. What a _____ enemy he had been! (submissive, powerful, formidable) _____

_____

7. I felt no sense of shame; only wild _____. (distaste, pleasure, exultation) _____

_____

8. I had fought this fish in his own environment—my strength against his strength—and I had _____. (fared well, won, triumphed) _____

_____

9. It was my very first meaningful _____ with Nature, and I would long remember it. (meeting, session, struggle) _____

_____

10. Now, as I study that beautiful sailfish mounted and displayed on the wall of my den, I give thanks that my first fish was so _____. (pusillanimous, bold, intrepid) _____

_____

Finished? Then read the "story" through, inserting the words you chose. In most cases you probably selected the third word in each set. You should feel just a little of the thrill that the amateur fisherman felt as he told this story!

Here's another experiment with the same story. Try reading it again, but this time insert the first word of each set. You will find it a totally different experience. The result is a different kind of fish story, one suitable for the self-mocking stage comic rather than for the boastful fisherman!

Read the story a third time, this time inserting the second word of each set. The result is again different—a fairly straightforward account of the incident, lacking in the excitement and thrill of the first reading and in the self-mockery of the second.

Words make the difference! Catching even a guppy can sound exciting if the story is properly told.

II. Activity

In the space below, write your own fish story. Make it as enthralling as you can, and use at least six of the words given in this chapter. When you have finished, switch stories with your classmates and enjoy a real old-fashioned fish story swapping bee!

4
First Flight

"Avis," the ancient Roman cried when he saw a bird fly above him. So when humans learned to fly (imitating the birds), they called themselves *avi*ators and the act of flying, *avi*ation. Naturally the place where birds are confined for display or study is an *aviary*, and the adjective used to describe characteristics suitable for birds is *avian*.

You have now taken the first step toward becoming an *ornithologist* (one who makes a scientific study of birds). Here are a few more steps.

I. There are 23 different birds in the square below. You can find them by moving from left to right, right to left, top to bottom, bottom to top, or diagonally. As you find each bird, circle it and enter its name on the list.

```
R H M S E T W F C Y S
E C O W L O R L R A W
P N C A T R E A A J O
I I K N A R N M N I O
P F I K W A H I E E D
D P N A C P O N A R P
N I G H T I N G A L E
A G B N O O L O W A C
S E I N D E S T O R K
R O R O B I N E R K E
K N D O V E K S C Y R
```

1. _____   13. _____

2. _____   14. _____

3. _____   15. _____

4. _____   16. _____

5. _____   17. _____

6. _____   18. _____

7. _____   19. _____

8. _____   20. _____

9. _____   21. _____

10. _____   22. _____

11. _____   23. _____

12. _____

II. Match some of the above 23 birds with the nonornithological definitions below:

1. one who is easily swindled (slang) _____

2. a crazy person _____

3. a pacifist _____

4. a machine for moving heavy objects _____

5. a dull, stupid person _____

6. one who favors a militaristic policy _____

7. one who repeats something without understanding it __ _____

8. a scoring term in golf _____

9. an informer (slang) _____

10. a harmless prank or adventure _____

III. Here are nine statements *about* birds. In the statements key words are italicized. Following the statements is a list of definitions. After each definition write the italicized word that best matches it.

1. Every color of the rainbow appears in the *plumage* of some bird.
2. An observer once watched a scarlet tanager *consume* 630 caterpillars in 18 minutes.
3. In the seasonal *migration* of birds, the bobolink each autumn travels 5,000 miles from the United States to Brazil.
4. Orioles tend to be *monogamous*, but turkeys and pheasants are *polygamous*.
5. The *repertoire* of the mockingbird often includes a dog's bark, the calls of other birds, and the sound of several musical instruments.
6. Each kind of bird prefers a certain kind of *habitat:* for example, meadow larks like open fields, while canyon wrens like caves.
7. Some birds—gulls, for instance—are *scavengers*, eating dead matter along the shore or from garbage heaps.
8. Some cuckoos are drab, while others are *iridescent*. Dull or bright, they lay their eggs in the nests of other birds, which immediately become foster parents.
9. The albatross is truly a *nomadic* bird, often spending weeks or even months at sea. It can sleep on the water and use seawater to quench its thirst.

a. displaying many bright colors _____

b. list of parts or pieces that an actor or singer can perform _____

c. the feathery covering of a bird _____

d. having more than one mate at a time _____

e. those who eat dead matter _____

f. wandering without a fixed residence _____

g. having only one mate _____

h. a periodic movement of a group from one region to another _____ *i.* the kind of place preferred by a particular kind of plant or animal _____

j. to use up; to devour _____

IV. Just for Fun

You are taking part in a kind of treasure hunt. Here are the names of 10 species of birds.

chickadee	mockingbird	tanager
finch	sparrow	warbler
herring gull	swallow	waxwing
lark		

Below are 10 things you are to find. You can find each of them in one of the birds listed above. Next to each "treasure," write the name of the bird in which you can find the treasure and circle the appropriate letters. For example, if you are asked to find a swine, you would write (PIG)EON.

1. Find the part of a fish that helps it to move. _____

2. Find a boat that provides safety. _____

3. Find a wornout horse. _____

4. Find a monarch. _____

5. Find a military conflict. _____

6. Find a partition between two rooms. _____

7. Find a fruit drink. _____

8. Find a piece of jewelry. _____

9. Find a pole or mast. _____

10. Find a hatchet. _____

V. To Test Your Deductive Powers

Complete each statement by inserting in each blank one of the words listed below.

avian	monogamy	plumage
habitat	nomadic	repertoire
migration		

1. The _____ of young people to Europe every summer is hurting parents' wallets.

2. In this country it is customary to have only one husband or wife at one time. Our laws insist on _____.

3. He entertained us for two hours. His _____ was varied and included song-and-dance routines, comedy sketches, and pantomimes.

4. Having the ability to fly without mechanical assistance is a(n) _____ characteristic.

5. Americans, ever more mobile, seldom live long in one community. We are becoming

   a(n) _____ people.

6. Some people prefer the city as their _____ ; others prefer open country.

7. As she left the house wearing her new spring outfit, someone commented on her fine

   _____.

5
The Insect World

Do you ignore insects—except to slap a mosquito or swat a fly? Then note this!

An *aphid* is a small, soft-bodied insect that sucks sap from plants. *One* aphid—*one*—can in a few weeks produce 6,000 million other aphids! Consider well that number: 6,000 million. It is almost completely beyond our understanding—a million 6,000 times!

To continue the story: That one aphid and its descendants in ten generations (equivalent to one summer) can produce so many aphids that their total weight would be equal to the weight of *all* the people living on the earth!* (To be honest, though, one must admit that this could occur only if none of this particular family were eaten or destroyed during the period, a situation that, we can thank our stars, is highly unlikely to happen.)

Do you still think it's wise to ignore insects?

The insect world is as varied in kind as it is *prolific* (capable of producing large numbers of offspring). More than 650,000 species of insects have been recognized and classified, but it is quite possible that an equal number of species exist that have not yet been found by human beings. Fortunately for us, most of these insects feed on other insects, thus keeping the insect population under control. If we are not aware of the balance of nature and the way it operates, we may have to stop speaking about the *insect world* and start speaking about the *insects' world!*

I. Here are five words related to insects:

   communal   metamorphosis   vampire
   insecticides   submerged

   Try to complete each of the following statements by inserting the word above that is most appropriate. (Don't forget to look for clues, and remember the process of elimination.)

   1. During the last couple of decades _____ have played havoc with the bee population.

   2. The caterpillar undergoes _____, or a complete change of form, in order to become a butterfly.

   3. Bedbugs are sometimes called _____ insects because they suck blood from humans in the dark of night.

   4. Water bugs live in lakes and ponds, and sometimes they lay their eggs on _____ objects, or objects beneath the surface.

   5. Ants and bees are members of a rigid caste system in which each individual creature depends on the group. For this reason ant and bee colonies provide fine working examples of _____ living.

II. Each of the next five sentences has two blanks for two missing words. After each sentence are two words. Place each word correctly in the sentence. Consult a dictionary when necessary.

   1. Since beetles feed on dead vegetable matter, they may be called _____;

*Figures from Professor Thomas Huxley.

since they also kill and feed on other insects, they may be called _ _ _ _ _ _ _ _ _ _ _ _ _ _ _ _ _.
(predatory, scavengers)

2. Since water beetles eat snails, fish, and other insects, they are properly called _ _ _ _ _ _ _ _

_ _ _ _ _ _ _ _ _ _ _ _ _ _ _ _ _; since they also eat a tremendous amount, they are correctly

described as _ _ _ _ _ _ _ _ _ _ _ _ _ _ _ _ _ _ _. (carnivorous; voracious)

3. The whirligig beetles that like both quiet water and running water are _ _ _ _ _ _ _ _ _ _ _ _ _

insects, while the hister beetles that prefer pastures are _

insects. (aquatic, terrestrial)

4. The moth is primarily _ _ _ _ _ _ _ _ _ _ _ _ _ _ _ _, while the butterfly, with which we are

all more familiar, is _ _ _ _ _ _ _ _ _ _ _ _ _ _ _ _ _. (diurnal, nocturnal)

5. Houseflies have one pair of wings that are _ _ _ _ _ _ _ _ _ _ _ _ _ _ _ _ _ _ _ and a pair of
knobbed, threadlike structures that were once wings and that now help them to

balance. The latter are properly called _. (functional, vestigial)

III. Insects have also influenced our language. The names of some insects have acquired a
second meaning. Can you match the insects in the first column with the second meanings
in the second column?

_ _ _ _ 1. caterpillar   *a.* small, hidden microphone used for eavesdropping

_ _ _ _ 2. wasp   *b.* frying pan on short legs

_ _ _ _ 3. bug   *c.* social gathering

_ _ _ _ 4. butterfly   *d.* parasite; one who clings to another

_ _ _ _ 5. leech   *e.* outdoor game popular in Great Britain; also, fairplay

_ _ _ _ 6. beetle   *f.* fishing lure

_ _ _ _ 7. spider   *g.* trademark for a tractor with endless chain treads

_ _ _ _ 8. cricket   *h.* person who is quick to take offense; an irritable person

_ _ _ _ 9. bee   *i.* Volkswagen automobile

_ _ _ _ 10. fly   *j.* frivolous pleasure-seeker

IV. **Four Facts and One Nonfact About Insects**

1. The male *dance fly*, when courting the female, not only finds her a gift of food but,
before presenting it, giftwraps it in a homemade web!
2. In the Orient, children nibble, as a special treat, on *diving beetles*.
3. The larva of the *drone fly* has a long, slender tube at the end of its body. When eating
under water, it sends up the "tail," which then serves as a snorkel air tube.
4. *Dragonflies* are sometimes called "the devil's darning needles" because they sew up the
ears of children who play hookey from school.
5. When the *driver ants* of Africa go on a raid, they devour not only other insects but any

trapped animals in their path. They have even been used to execute slaves and political prisoners.

Now can you answer the following questions?

a. Which of the above passages (1, 2, 3, 4, or 5) is a nonfact, or a *legend* handed down from earlier times? ____

b. Which passage would interest a lover of *aquatic* sports? ____

c. Which might interest a *gourmet*? ____

d. Which would appeal to a *barbarous* or *brutal* person? ____

e. Which would appeal to a *sentimental* person? ____

V. Activity

Choose any three of the insects named in Exercise III. In paragraph form, suggest a reason why each of the three names acquired its second meaning.

6
Larking With Livestock

Farms are fine places to learn about *domesticated* animals, animals raised to be useful to man. Within 30 minutes on a farm, you can see a calf nuzzling its mother for milk, sheep grazing peacefully in a pasture, horses peering curiously from the stable, and pigs grunting noisily for a second breakfast. But farms can be confusing places if you don't know the terminology in daily use.

I. Friends and Relations

Analogies (statements of resemblance in some particulars between things otherwise unlike) are helpful in understanding relationships. Suppose you are given this analogy: "A hen is to a chick as a cow is to a _____ (bull, calf)." You must first ask yourself what the relationship is between a hen and a chick. You decide it is that of mother to offspring. Your next question concerns the second half of the analogy: What is the offspring of a cow called? Obviously the answer is "calf." You choose the second word in parentheses, "calf," and your analogy is complete. How many of the following analogies can you complete correctly?

1. A cow is to a bull as a ewe is to a _____ . (lamb, ram)

2. A cow is to a calf as a ewe is to a _____ . (lamb, ram)

3. A herd is to a cow as a flock is to a _____ . (pig, sheep)

4. A pig is to a sty as a pigeon is to a _____ . (cote, pasture)

5. "To calve" is to a cow as "to lamb" is to a _____ . (ewe, ram)

6. A sow is to a hen as a boar is to a _____ . (ram, rooster)

7. A nanny goat is to a kid as a goose is to a _____ . (gander, gosling)

8. A goose is to a gander as a duck is to a _____ . (drake, duckling)

9. A pigeon is to a squab as a horse is to a _____ . (foal, mule)

10. A pig is to a squeal as a horse is to a _____ . (bleat, neigh)

II. Animal Masks

Because farm animals are so common and their habits so well known, their names have often become associated with certain types of people. Below are ten animal *epithets*, terms used to characterize persons or things. After each one, explain the reason for the use of that particular epithet.

Example: "Bill is a hog," Sue said disapprovingly as her brother took the last two slices of cake.

A hog has a reputation for eating a great deal, even more than it may need. Since Bill is eating too much cake, he is acting like a hog.

Here are 10 animal epithets for you to try.

1. "I don't mind taking care of the baby; she's a *lamb*," the baby-sitter said. "But I can't

stand the older kids." _____

_____

_____

2. Jerry refused to go to the doctor, but then he has always been a *mule*. _____

_____

_____

3. "Jenny's some *chick*!" the male chauvinist said between whistles. _____

_____

_____

4. Keep Jim out of the kitchen. He's like a *bull* in a china shop! _____

_____

_____

5. "My brother plays the piano and my sister writes poetry. All I do is get into trouble!"
Rick grumbled. "I guess you could say that I'm the *black sheep* of the family." _____

_____

6. "Children are *pigs*!" she said as she stalked from the table. _____

_____

_____

7. The politician angrily called the voters a flock of *sheep*. _____

_____

_____

8. After watching the student demonstration for a few minutes, Mr. Jones' eyes focused
on his son. "It's easy to see who the *bellwether* is," he muttered. _____

_____

_____

9. "I acted like a *silly goose*," Helen said ruefully. "I just spent my whole allowance on a
beautiful leash—and I don't even own a dog!" _____

_____

_____

10. "I can't get along with my next-door neighbor, Mrs. Perry," Margie complained.
"She's a cantankerous old *hen*." _____

_____

_____

III. Horse-Trading

Horses are *perennial* (everlasting; appearing again and again) favorites with young people. Here's a chance to select your "dream horse."

A. **The Horse Family**: Match the family member in the first column with the description in the second column. Then place a check in the box at the left of the term that matches your dream horse.

☐ ____ 1. filly   *a.* female horse

☐ ____ 2. stallion   *b.* young female horse

☐ ____ 3. colt   *c.* a young horse of either sex, especially one less than a year old

☐ ____ 4. mare   *d.* male horse

☐ ____ 5. foal   *e.* young male horse

B. **Colors**: Match the colors in the first column with their definitions in the second. Then place a check in the box next to the color of your dream horse.

☐ ____ 1. chestnut   *a.* brownish gray to grayish brown

☐ ____ 2. strawberry roan   *b.* brownish orange to light brown

☐ ____ 3. bay   *c.* grayish to reddish brown

☐ ____ 4. sorrel   *d.* red sprinkled with gold and white hairs

☐ ____ 5. dun   *e.* reddish brown with black mane, tail, and points

C. **Height**: A horse is usually measured by "hands." How big is a "hand"? (*a*) four inches; (*b*) eight inches; (*c*) twelve inches; (*d*) two feet; (*e*) one yard ____

Keeping your answer in mind, insert in the blank the height in "hands" of your dream horse. ____

D. **Kinds of Horses**: This time match the kind of horse in the first column with the description of the horse in the second column. (Note: *Conformation* means the structure or outline of an animal or thing.) Then place a check in the box next to the kind that most closely matches your dream horse.

☐ ____ 1. palomino

☐ ____ 2. thoroughbred

☐ ____ 3. Arabian

☐ ____ 4. Percheron

☐ ____ 5. Shetland

a. A draft horse, usually gray or black. Conformation: heavy bones and muscles, deep and wide chest, low-set body.

b. A pony, usually about 40 inches high. Conformation: sturdy legs, round body, short neck and head.

c. A race horse. Conformation: long, slender body, good muscles, long neck, long legs, large expressive eyes.

d. A horse with endurance; oldest breed of horse living today. Conformation: short back, wedge-shaped head, arched neck. Spirited.

e. A golden-colored horse, Spanish stock. Conformation: general fine appearance, but emphasis is on color.

You now know all you need to know (well, almost) about buying a horse. Of course, you still need money, a place to keep the horse, someone to take care of it, etc. Otherwise—your dream horse is within reach!

IV. To Test Your Deductive Powers

Insert one of the following five words in each blank in the sentences below:

analogy   domesticate   perennial
conformation   epithet

1. Many gardeners prefer to plant a(n) _ because it comes up year after year.

2. In discussions, it is sometimes helpful to use a(n) _ to clarify a difficult relationship.

3. To _ a wild animal, one must be prepared to expend both time and patience.

4. The _ "cold" in the phrase "cold war" is, to put it mildly, curious—as John F. Kennedy once noted.

5. Phrenologists claim that they can tell a great deal about a person from the _ _ _ _ _ _ _ _ _ _
_ _ _ _ _ _ _ _ _ _ _ _ _ of his head.

7
Peripatetic* Pets

Would you like to *patter* through the *P* section of the dictionary *probing* for *peripatetic pets?*

Each cluster below contains several definitions. At the right of each definition, write the word defined. Then copy the circled letters on the last line of the cluster and you will have found a pet. In all, there are 10 pets. At the end of the 10 clusters is a glossary of 54 words all beginning with P, and all dealing with animals or their training.

Cluster 1

1. plump game bird found at Christmas "in a pear tree"   1. P_ _ _ _ _ _Ⓞ_ _

2. small horse   2. PⓄ_ _

3. record of ancestry of a purebred animal   3. P_ _ _ _Ⓞ_ _ _

   Pet: _ _ _ _

Cluster 2

1. to shoot game or catch fish in a forbidden area   1. P_ _ _Ⓞ_

2. something essential when you begin to housebreak a pet   2. PⓄ_ _ _

3. hunting dog with a short-haired coat   3. P_ _ _ _Ⓞ_ _

   Pet: _ _ _ _

Cluster 3

1. general term for the equipment you need for your pet   1. P_ _ _ _Ⓞ_ _ _ _ _ _

2. foot of an animal   2. PⓄ_

3. golden-colored horse with creamy mane   3. P_ _ _ _Ⓞ_ _ _

4. having the quiet and charm of country life   4. P_Ⓞ_ _ _ _

5. feeling remorse; the way you will feel if you mistreat your pet   5. P_ _ _ _ _ _ _Ⓞ

6. animal victim of another animal   6. P_Ⓞ_

7. animal that preys on another animal   7. P_ _ _ _ _ _Ⓞ

   Pet: _ _ _ _ _ _ _ _

Peripatetic means "walking around; wandering."

Cluster 4

1. food element that helps animal tissue to grow and is necessary for humans and most pets

2. harmonious state achieved when pets fall asleep at night

3. what food must be if your pet is to eat it

4. strain resulting after breeding unmixed stock for many generations

5. pitiful; the way a pet looks when it is neglected

6. animal skin

Pet: _____

1. P⊖_____
2. P__⊖___
3. P_____⊖__
4. P____⊖____
5. P_____⊖_
6. P__⊖

Cluster 5

1. quality you need to train any pet

2. once a shepherd of sheep; now a spiritual shepherd

3. pad behind the saddle of a horse; serves as seat for an extra rider

4. A pet can be one.

5. to overindulge; to cater to

6. frequent mood for most pets

Pet: _____

1. P_____⊖_
2. P⊖_____
3. P_____⊖
4. P⊖_
5. P_____⊖
6. P__⊖___

Cluster 6

1. unusual or strange trait in animals or humans

2. small dog with snub nose and square body

3. Gain, or return. You will expect this if you breed pets as a business.

4. to repeat without understanding, like a particular tropical bird

5. result of a small catastrophe with a puppy

6. feathers of a bird

Pet: _____

1. P_____⊖_
2. P⊖_
3. P⊖_____
4. P_____⊖
5. P____⊖_
6. P_____⊖

Cluster 7

1. pertaining to fish and fishing
2. enclosure where stray dogs and cats are confined
3. short quick gasps that occur after hard running
4. fenced area for pasturing or exercising horses
5. to clean or smooth feathers

   Pet: _ _ _ _ _ _

1. P _ _ Ⓞ _ _ _ _ _ _ _ _
2. P _ _ _ Ⓞ _
3. P Ⓞ _ _ _
4. P _ _ _ _ _ _ Ⓞ
5. P _ Ⓞ _ _

Cluster 8

1. producing offspring in abundance
2. spotted horse or pony
3. grasslands for grazing animals
4. pocket in which marsupials carry their young

   Pet: _ _ _ _ _

1. P _ _ _ _ _ Ⓞ _ _
2. P Ⓞ _ _ _
3. P _ Ⓞ _ _ _
4. P _ _ _ _ Ⓞ

Cluster 9

1. soft, high-pitched cry of a baby bird
2. bearlike mammal from China
3. domestic fowls, e.g., chickens and turkeys
4. what will look attractive in your aquarium
5. flesh of a pig
6. upper front part of a saddle; also a verb meaning "to beat"
7. fenced enclosure for some animals, e.g., bulls or pigs
8. distinctive traits of a person or animal

   Pet: _ _ _ _ _ _ _ _ _

1. P _ _ Ⓞ
2. P Ⓞ _ _ _
3. P _ _ _ _ _ Ⓞ _
4. P _ Ⓞ _ _ _ _
5. P _ _ Ⓞ
6. P _ _ _ _ Ⓞ _
7. P Ⓞ _
8. P _ _ _ _ _ _ _ _ _ _ Ⓞ _

Cluster 10

1. young dog
2. bird's wing
3. flying horse in Greek mythology
4. small dog with thick, curly hair
5. nickname for a parrot
6. hair style in which hair is caught together and tied in the back

   Pet: _ _ _ _ _ _ _ _

1. P _ Ⓞ _ _
2. P _ _ Ⓞ _ _
3. P _ Ⓞ _ _ _ _
4. P _ _ _ _ _ Ⓞ
5. P Ⓞ _ _ _
6. P _ Ⓞ _ _ _ _ _

Glossary

paddock	peculiarity	pommel
pal	pedigree	pony
palatable	peep	ponytail
palomino	Pegasus	poodle
pamper	pelt	pork
panda	pen	pouch
pants	penitent	poultry
paper	personality	pound
paraphernalia	pillion	predator
parrot	pinion	preen
partridge	pinto	prey
pastor	piscatorial	profit
pastoral	plants	prolific
pasture	playful	protein
pathetic	plumage	puddle
patience	poach	pug
paw	pointer	puppy
peace	Polly	purebred

8
Mammalian (and Non-mammalian) Mysteries

I. Murder on the March

Tex Pym and Tod Pom had been business rivals for years, but they were also known as good friends, since they often met socially. Last summer the two men decided to go on a safari. In Africa they bought a jeep, filled it with equipment, and set out.

A week later Tod Pom, alone, drove wearily into a large town. He had a horrible tale to tell. A couple of days earlier he and Tex had come across a large elephant. Tex had fired and wounded the animal, but the elephant had promptly charged him.

Tod shuddered at this point. "That great carnivorous beast—that devil-mammoth—it—" He stopped, sobbing, then continued. "It—it knocked Tex down and trampled on him. It pushed him around with its tusks, and finally it—" He shuddered again. "Finally it *ate* him! Poor Tex!"

He waited, expecting to feel a sympathetic hand on his shoulder. Instead he heard the jangle of handcuffs. "O.K., Pom," the chief of police said grimly, "we know you murdered Pym!"

How did the chief know Tod was lying?

II. Hanged by an Alibi

Judge Fox called the court to order. His eyes gleamed maliciously as he studied the three suspects lined up before him: Mrs. Robin, Mrs. Cuckoo, and Mrs. Chickadee.

"All right, ladies," he said firmly. "One of you stole grain from Farmer Jones at 11:25 this morning. Does anyone have an alibi?"

"I have," the three women said simultaneously. It turned out that the three birds had the same alibi: each insisted she had been in her nest at 11:25 A.M., sitting on her eggs.

Although all three had the same alibi, Judge Fox immediately knew which one was lying. Which of the three suspects did he charge with the crime, and on what basis did he make his decision?

III. The Wild West

It was a hot July morning when two cowboys rode up to the sheriff's office.

"I was riding on my palomino," the first cowboy said to the sheriff, "and that guy shot me." He shrugged. "He says it was an accident, and maybe it was. Anyway, I'm not much hurt—just my shoulder, my leg, and my chest."

The second cowboy looked sheepish. "Like he said, Sheriff—it was an accident. He was riding in front of a bunch of green trees, and with that green shirt he kind of blended into the background. I didn't see him—honest, I didn't. I was just shooting at a buzzard."

The sheriff grabbed the second cowboy. "I can't stand a liar," he snarled. "Especially a stupid liar!"

How did the sheriff know that the shooting was no accident?

IV. Scrambled Animals

Since the Zany Zoo and the Amazing Amusement Park were enemies, their collectors were careful to communicate in code. Mr. Zinch called the Zany Zoo and told them to expect a telegram. "I'm bringing back 13 mammals, 5 fish (including two shellfish), 2 birds, and 1 insect," he said.

Here's the telegram the Zany Zoo received the next day.

Dear Aunt Mar,

All is calm here, but I'm feeling a bit low. Karl found a wee leaf on the shore, but someone managed to stab him with a reed. He recovered, and we dined on a loaf of bread, a green pea, and three wines. Then I wrote an ode about a star while he extracted nails from a loin of pork that we uncovered on the lee side of the island. The pork harks back to 1776. It was lying under a ream of paper and was protected by balm.

Love,
Zinchie

Can you decode the underlined words in the telegram and find all the creatures that Mr. Zinch had collected? *Example:* In the first line aunt can be unscrambled to become tuna. (Note: Two words are plural in form.) As you decode them, insert the names in the columns on the next page.

Mammals	Fish	Birds	Insect
---------------	---------------	---------------	---------------
---------------	---------------	---------------	
---------------	---------------		
---------------	---------------		
---------------	---------------		

Six. The Last Word About Sports

1

Ball Barrage

List them: baseball, football, and polo; basketball and billiards; tennis and ping pong and volleyball; cricket and handball; croquet and soccer; bowling and golf.

The one thing they all have in common is that they are played with—a *ball*.

When did ball-playing start? The truth is that no one knows. Two thousand years ago the Greeks and Romans played ball just for fun; 3,000 years ago a ball and a stick were used together in some kind of game; 4,000 years ago (according to a painting in an Egyptian tomb) women tossed a ball back and forth as a means of relaxation.

Probably ball-playing is even older than these records indicate. Ball-playing was part of religious ceremonies at one time; it may have been a *rite* (a ceremony; an act with a prescribed form) designed to bring rain; it may have been a substitute for war and personal combat; it may have been part of a test to determine which man was the strongest and most courageous. Quite possibly it was all of these.

History tells us of an unusual "trial by combat"—an ordeal to determine which side is good, which evil. Ardashir I, ruler of Persia, used this method in 230 A.D. to prove the legitimacy of his son. The "combat" was a huge polo game with a thousand or more men on each team! And we think the 20th century is the age of spectaculars!

Times have not changed that much. Though ball-playing is no longer part of formal religion, its ancestry helps to explain the fanatic intensity of sports fans. Who else but a football *fan*atic would spend New Year's Day plastered to a TV set for eight hours? Who else but a baseball *fan*atic would sit under the merciless August sun for a doubleheader?

Any part of life that means so much to so many has to influence all of life. Certainly it has to influence language.

I. The Ballplayers' Dictionary

Here is a short glossary of sports words:

fumble: to mishandle a ground ball; to drop a ball
pinch hitter: a substitute batter called in when a hit is badly needed
quarterback: the player who calls the signals for the plays
squeeze play: a play in which a batter tries a bunt so that a runner on third base may score
tackle: to grab an opponent and bring him to the ground in order to stop him

Below are five passages *not* related to sports. After each passage explain briefly what the sports term means in that particular passage and why the writer probably used it.

1. As he reached a critical point in his speech, he realized that one *fumble* now would completely destroy his team's chance of winning the debate.

----

2. The spelling bee was almost over. Jody listened to the new word, realized he couldn't spell it, and wished desperately that he could call in a *pinch hitter*.

----

3. During a war, after each major battle there are more Sunday-morning *quarterbacks* in this country than there are soldiers in the army.

----

4. Spy Harry knew he had to give Spy Johnnie a chance to get beyond the enemy lines with the microfilm they had captured. But how? Ah, the old *squeeze play*, of course! Shooting madly, Harry darted from his hiding place, and as the enemy fire centered on him, his partner slipped to safety.

----

5. Although he dreaded the prospect, Will knew that sooner or later he would have to *tackle* the job of fixing the washing machine.

II. Here's a barrage of balls. If you can field between 8 and 10 of them, you make the varsity team. If you can field 5 to 7, you make junior varsity. If you fumble 7 or more, you're benched forever! To field a ball, insert each of the 10 listed words in the sentence in which it is most appropriate.

agility	invincible	precision
aura	nullified	strategy
charisma	ordeal	tactics
chore		

Football

1. "Whatever chance the Browns had of coming back in the second half went flying when

a penalty _____ (*cancelled; made useless*) a good gain and a good drive." (Cameron C. Snyder, *Baltimore Sun*)

2. ". . . _____ (*plan of action*) determines what is to be done and _____

_____ (*techniques*) are the means employed to do it." (Jim Moore, *Major Sports Techniques Illustrated*)

Baseball

3. "As an everyday _____ (*routine task*) with the Yankees, Mantle autographs six dozen balls when he first reports to the locker room." (Blackie Sherrod, *Dallas Times Herald*)

4. "The Cardinals finally ended their _____ (*difficult test or experience*) when Lolich struck out after an intentional walk to Don Wert." (Joseph Durso, *New York Times*)

Basketball

5. "The Bruins, who had been committing turnover after turnover . . . quickly congealed into a team of _____ (*exactness; efficiency*) and force." (Dwight Chapin, *Los Angeles Times*)

6. "Of all the players, though, the overwhelming favorite is Walt Frazier, a slender, muscular athlete whose presence on the court is dramatized by his quickness and

   _____ (*nimbleness; ability to move quickly and easily*)." (Peter Bonventre, *McCalls Magazine*)

Golf

7. "Palmer is the most daring, aggressive player in the game today, and there is a(n)

   _____ (*air, quality*) of the _____ (*unconquerable*) about him because he storms from behind to win again and again." (Jack Murphy, *San Diego Union*)

8. "For sheer _____ (*the quality of winning the admiration of many people*), no other golfer even comes close to Palmer . . . ." (William Murray, *Playboy*)

III. **Bowling**

One of the oldest ball games of all is bowling, which was providing happy competition to Egyptians 7,000 years ago. That's right, 7,000! When Julius Caesar ruled the Roman Empire, Italians were playing "boccie," or lawn bowling. A few hundred years later, members of the congregation were bowling in European churches to separate the strong and faithful from the weak and sinful. The Puritans, who seldom played at all, did play at ninepins. Finally, in the 19th century, when ninepins was banned because of the gambling and corruption that surrounded it, tenpins—or modern bowling—was born.

Now try this ball barrage:

coordination	follow-through	stance
etiquette	pendulum	

1. The first thing to remember when you bowl is that your _____, or position of the feet, is exceedingly important.

2. After the release of the ball, your arm motion should provide smooth and effective

   _____.

3. You swing the ball back, then forward, in what is logically known as a _ _ _ _ _ _ _ _ _ _ _ _

_ _ _ _ _ _ _ _ _ _ _ _ _ swing.

4. Bowling, like most sports, demands the _ of several basic actions into one complex skill.

5. The _ of bowling requires that a player wait his turn, that he not waste time posing, and that he not use another player's ball without permission.

2
Racquet Squad

The Master-Devil sat in his jacket,
And all the souls were playing at racket.
No other rackets they had in hand,
Save every soul a good firebrand.

Wherewith they played so prettily,
That Lucifer laughed merrily;
And all the residue of the fiends
Did laugh full well together like friends.

from John Heywood's *The Four P's*, 1540

I. Spell it *racquet* or *racket*, it makes little difference. Either way, there are plenty of rackets to go around. There's the racquet with an elliptical hoop strung with catgut and used in

------------------ ; there's the racquet that is lighter, slightly smaller, with a long

handle used in ------------------ ; and there's the small wooden-paddle racquet used

in ------------------ . There are other rackets, too: the racket that is a lot of noise and uproar; the racket that is an illegal and fraudulent business; and the racket that is an easy, "snap" job.

II. The racquet games—tennis, table tennis (or ping-pong), badminton, squash, and lacrosse—share more than the use of the racquet. They all require certain skills or talents. Try to match the traits in the first column with the definitions in the second.

---- 1. dexterity   *a.* exactness; correctness

---- 2. endurance   *b.* quickness to perceive and act

---- 3. accuracy   *c.* perseverance in spite of hardships

---- 4. mobility   *d.* bodily or manual skill

---- 5. alertness   *e.* ability to move quickly

There are a few other things racquet-wielders need. Continue by matching the adjectives (italicized words) in the first column with the definitions in the second.

---- 6. *phenomenal* speed   *f.* showy; marked by dashing display

---- 7. *flamboyant* play   *g.* overwhelming; crushing

---- 8. *crisp* volleys   *h.* extraordinary; remarkable

---- 9. *arduous* preparation   *i.* brisk; lively

---- 10. *annihilating* service   *j.* strenuous; very difficult

III. **Detecting With the Dictionary and Deduction**

1. Why is ping-pong called ping-pong? (*Clue:* Think of the two points of contact made by the ball.)

---

2. What is a "lob" in tennis?

---

3. Why is badminton called badminton? (*Clue:* Consult the dictionary, and then deduce.)

---

4. Why might a cynic say that *love* is best described by its meaning in tennis? (*Clue:* Check the meaning of *love* in tennis; check the meaning of *cynic;* then think!)

---

5. From what Arabic word is the word *racquet* derived? What did it originally mean? Can you suggest a possible relationship between the present meaning and the original meaning?

---

6. What is the difference between *court tennis* and *lawn tennis*?

---

7. What is the Davis Cup, and how did it get its name?

---

8. "A tennis ball is an inflated, hermetically sealed rubber sphere covered with stitchless felt cloth." What does *hermetically sealed* mean?

---

9. Badminton is played with a shuttlecock rather than a ball. Describe a shuttlecock. What else is it called?

---

10. "When playing a racquet game, try to *anticipate* shots and keep a *supple* wrist." Explain the two directions given.

IV. Activity

Write a paragraph describing a sports event in which you participated or which you watched. Use nouns like *mobility* and *endurance* and adjectives like *flamboyant* and *crisp* to make your writing vivid.

3
To the Swift

To begin, write a brief paragraph about a race—any kind of race: a footrace of 10-year-olds, an auto race, a motorcycle race, a horserace.

Now, on the lines below write all the verbs (action words) that you used in the paragraph.

--------------------   --------------------   --------------------

--------------------   --------------------   --------------------

--------------------   --------------------   --------------------

--------------------   --------------------   --------------------

Study the words for a minute. Are they vivid, colorful, alive? Do they express speed and tension? Do they create suspense?

I. The world of racing is a world of action. If you want to describe a race well, you must have strong action verbs at the point of your pen.

In a recent auto race, five drivers performed certain actions:

1. Driver "A" *drove closely behind* another car.
2. Driver "B" *increased speed* madly.
3. Driver "C" *moved with a loud noise* around the track.
4. Driver "D" *drove with force* into a pileup.
5. Driver "E" *slowed down with a prolonged shrill noise* to a halt.

Rewrite each sentence, replacing the italicized phrase with one of these action words: *accelerated, plowed, roared, screeched, tailgated.*

1. --

2. --

3. --

4. --

5. --

II. In a recent horserace, four horses moved in certain ways.

1. Horses Harriet, Harry, Henry, and Hilda *moved with dull, heavy sounds* past the grandstand.
2. Horse Henry *moved ineptly* and faded to fourth place.
3. Horse Harry *reduced sharply* Horse Hilda's lead.
4. Horse Harriet *appeared in a threatening way* behind Horse Harry.
5. Horse Hilda *moved with force and violence* across the finish line.

Rewrite each sentence, replacing the italicized phrase with one of these action expressions: *charged, faltered, loomed ominously, slashed away at, thudded.*

1. _____

2. _____

3. _____

4. _____

5. _____

III. **Champions' Choice**

The words in the first column below are the actual names of thoroughbred champions, but they also have less equestrian (pertaining to horsemanship) meanings. Match each word with its nonequestrian definition.

____	1. Citation	*a.*	tramp; wanderer
____	2. Cicada	*b.*	anyone from whom a person is descended
____	3. Bayou	*c.*	ceremonial procession
____	4. Vagrant	*d.*	official commendation or approval
____	5. Delegate	*e.*	agent; representative
____	6. Centurion	*f.*	marshy body of water
____	7. Ancestor	*g.*	rectangular area with buildings on all four sides
____	8. Assault	*h.*	insect that emits a high-pitched sound
____	9. Cavalcade	*i.*	officer in the Roman army
____	10. Quadrangle	*j.*	violent attack

IV. Here are the names of five more thoroughbreds. Suggest a probable reason why the owner of each horse chose that particular name.

1. Fleet Shoe _____

_____

2. High Quest _____

_____

3. Money Broker _____

_____

4. High Echelon _____

_____

5. Crafty Admiral _____

_____

V. Measurements are especially important in races of all kinds. In a dictionary, find definitions of these units of measurement.

1. meter: _____

2. length: _____

3. furlong: _____

4. nose: _____

5. kilometer: _____

Using the definitions that you found, answer the following questions:

6. If a horse wins a four-furlong race, has he run (a) $\frac{1}{4}$ mile (b) $\frac{1}{2}$ mile (c) 1 mile? ____

7. If a runner wins a 100-meter race, has he run approximately (a) 110 yards (b) 550 yards (c) 1,000 yards? ____

8. If a skier wins the 15-kilometer race, has he covered (a) 1 mile (b) 9 miles (c) 15 miles? ____

9. If a horse wins by a length, has he won by (a) five inches (b) five feet (c) five yards? ____

10. If a horse wins by a nose, has he won by (a) a few inches (b) a few feet (c) a few yards? ____

VI. Some racing terms are so popular that they are used to describe nonathletic, nonracing events. First be sure you know what they mean in connection with racing.

1. *Hurdles* are the barriers used in obstacle races.
2. *Lap* is a complete circuit in a race or one segment of a race.
3. *Marathon* is a contest requiring endurance. It is usually long, in time or in distance.
4. *Photo finish* is a race so closely contested that a photograph is used to determine the winner.
5. *Relay* is a word used to describe the action when one person or team relieves another in orderly fashion.

You have probably heard all five of these terms used in connection with races. Now write sentences using three of them in nonathletic ways. Be sure, however, that you use the word as it is defined above.

The Last Word About Sports

1. --
   ----
2. --
   ----
3. --

4
In the Saddle

You have already learned something about horses (in Part Five, Chapter 6), but there is a great deal more to know about this perennial favorite.

I. Begin acquiring equestrian knowledge by trying to identify the parts of the horse shown below. Here are the terms you will need:

croup   hoof   muzzle
fetlock   loins   nape
haunch   mane   withers
hock

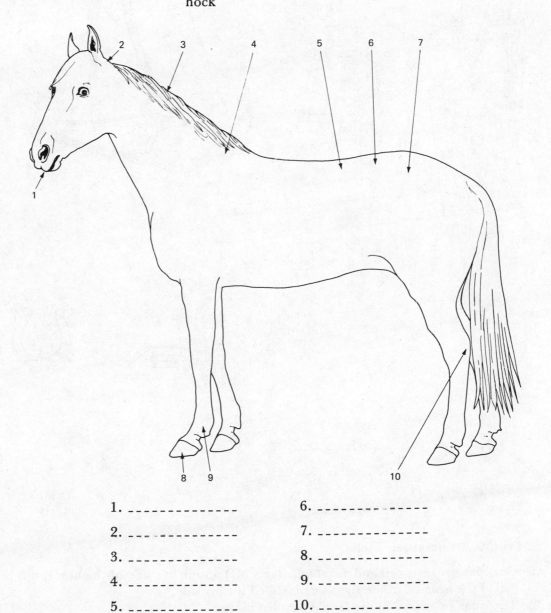

1. _ _ _ _ _ _ _ _ _ _ _ _ _   6. _ _ _ _ _ _ _ _ _ _ _ _ _

2. _ _ _ _ _ _ _ _ _ _ _ _ _   7. _ _ _ _ _ _ _ _ _ _ _ _ _

3. _ _ _ _ _ _ _ _ _ _ _ _ _   8. _ _ _ _ _ _ _ _ _ _ _ _ _

4. _ _ _ _ _ _ _ _ _ _ _ _ _   9. _ _ _ _ _ _ _ _ _ _ _ _ _

5. _ _ _ _ _ _ _ _ _ _ _ _ _   10. _ _ _ _ _ _ _ _ _ _ _ _ _

II. In the tack room, one finds the equipment (or "tack") used for horseback riding: the *bit*, the *bridle*, the *reins*, the *saddle* (including the *pommel* and the *cantle*), the *shoe*, and the *stirrup*. Continue acquiring equestrian knowledge by identifying the above:

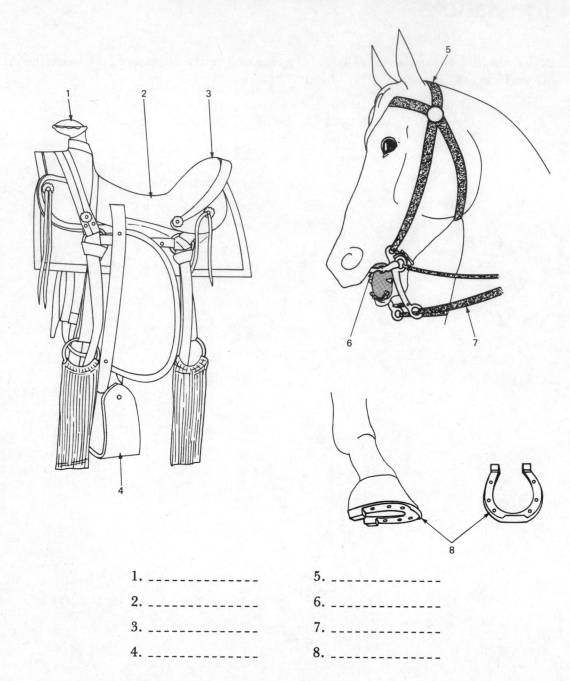

1. _ _ _ _ _ _ _ _ _ _ _ _ _   5. _ _ _ _ _ _ _ _ _ _ _ _ _

2. _ _ _ _ _ _ _ _ _ _ _ _ _   6. _ _ _ _ _ _ _ _ _ _ _ _ _

3. _ _ _ _ _ _ _ _ _ _ _ _ _   7. _ _ _ _ _ _ _ _ _ _ _ _ _

4. _ _ _ _ _ _ _ _ _ _ _ _ _   8. _ _ _ _ _ _ _ _ _ _ _ _ _

III. A Few More Equestrian Facts

1. One *mounts* (gets on) and *dismounts* (gets off) on the left side of the horse; this is called the *near* side. The right side is called the *off* side.
2. The rider's position in the saddle is called his *seat*.

3. The rider speaks to the horse through his *hands*, his *legs*, his *back*, his *weight*, and his *voice*.

4. There are five *gaits*, or ways of walking or running, that a horse generally uses:

> the slowest is the *walk;*
>
> a little faster than the walk is the *trot;*
>
> faster still is the *canter;*
>
> very fast, indeed, is the *gallop;*
>
> and the fastest of all is the *run.*

(*Note:* *Canter* comes from Canterbury gallop, because the pilgrims going to Canterbury rode at this pace.)

IV. A Horsey Set*

Match the 10 horse-related words and phrases in the first column with the definitions in the second. (Verb forms are expressed as infinitives, e.g., *to* saddle.)

____	1. stirrup cup	*a.*	to exercise close control over
____	2. bridle path	*b.*	in a dominant position
____	3. to bridle	*c.*	farewell drink for a rider who has already mounted
____	4. to keep a tight rein on	*d.*	leather pouch
____	5. to give free rein to	*e.*	to show resentment; to become angry
____	6. pommel	*f.*	to place a burden upon
____	7. in the saddle	*g.*	trail for saddle horses
____	8. to saddle	*h.*	knob at the front and top of a saddle
____	9. saddlebag	*i.*	to loosen controls completely
____	10. to muzzle	*j.*	to stop someone from expressing an opinion

V. Broncobuster

A broncobuster is a cowboy who breaks broncos (or wild horses) and trains them to accept the saddle. Here are two herds of broncos that need busting!

A. To satisfy each definition below in the second column, complete the "horse" word in the first column. The number of blanks corresponds to the number of letters missing.

1. horse_____	1. a baseball
2. horse_____	2. rowdy, noisy fooling around
3. horse_____	3. loud, mocking guffaw
4. horse_____	4. shrewd deal
5. horse _____	5. western film (2 words)

*People who are extremely interested in horses and horsemanship.

6. horse＿ ＿ ＿

6. large insect; one that sucks the blood of mammals

7. horse＿＿＿＿＿＿

7. sharp, spicy condiment

8. horse ＿＿＿＿＿

8. down-to-earth judgment (2 words)

9. horse＿＿＿ ＿＿＿＿＿＿

9. automobile (2 words)

10. horse＿＿＿＿

10. kind of cloth used in upholstery

B. After each of the sentences below, explain briefly the meaning of the italicized phrase:

1. *Hold your horses*, Joe! In a minute we'll be there!

----

2. Don't *get on your high horse* with me, Tony. I knew you when you didn't have two nickels to rub against each other!

----

3. Don't believe the newspaper story if you don't want to. Go get the information *from the horse's mouth*. Maybe then you'll believe it!

----

4. If only I had known you were ill yesterday. That's *a horse of a different color*, after all.

----

5. Jack Schwartz was the *dark horse* of the convention. His nomination came as a surprise to all.

5

Snow Magic

Take a city street that is gray with soot and dark with litter, sprinkle with a few inches of snow, and—presto!—a Currier and Ives print.

Or take a good-sized hill, cover it with the same frozen stuff, and watch the farmer's debit turn into a popular, money-making ski slope.

Snow has, for centuries, been considered magical. Poets have noted with awe its softness, its purity, its crystal-like nature; artists have tried hopelessly to capture the delicate complexity of one snowflake; lovers have revelled in its ability to provide solitude even when they are in a crowd. But only in our own time has another magical attribute of snow been discovered: it is almost as effective as a mint for making money.

An increase in leisure time has meant an increase in leisure-time activities, and with the coming of ice and snow, that means winter sports.

I. Skiing

Skiing isn't new. Swedish soldiers skied into battle in the year 1200, and mailmen skied to deliver letters to gold miners in 1849. But skiing as a sport here in the U.S.A. didn't really get started until the 1930's. The one essential piece of equipment is, of course, the pair of skis.

The paragraph below describes some of the things you should know about skis. Following the paragraph is a mini-glossary. From the glossary select an appropriate term for each blank.

Some skis are made of solid hickory, some of (1) _____

hickory. All skis should be (2)_____ rather than rigid. Most

skis should be waxed to protect them from (3) _____, but

wooden skis should first be varnished to prevent (4) _____
by moisture. Steel edges on the skis improve the grip, but in the event of a fall, they can

also cause serious (5) _____.

Glossary

abrasions—scraped or bruised areas
deterioration—act of growing worse, of decreasing in quality
flexible—capable of being bent, of bending
lacerations—jagged wounds; tears
laminated—composed of thin layers bonded together

II. Ice Skating

Here are five statements about skating.

1. In "show skating" women rather than men are likely to win international *acclaim*.
2. A beginning skater is primarily concerned with maintaining his *equilibrium*.
3. Later the same skater will seek to acquire increased *momentum* on the ice.
4. After learning the basic *maneuvers*, many skaters go on to figure skating.
5. Some psychiatrists have suggested that patients take up skating as a form of *therapy*.

Now try to match the italicized words with their definitions:

---- 1. acclaim   *a.* physical, mental, or emotional balance

---- 2. equilibrium   *b.* a continuing motion resulting from speed

---- 3. momentum   *c.* treatment of illness

---- 4. maneuvers   *d.* applause

---- 5. therapy   *e.* movements that require skill

III. Other winter sports include ice hockey, sledding, snowshoeing, ice boating, and curling. Since all these activities, from skiing to curling, are fast and light, certain verbs are used again and again in descriptions and reports. Five of the most popular are COAST, GLIDE, SKID, SKIM, and SWOOP. Below are five clusters of sentences. The three sentences in each cluster can all be completed by inserting the *same* word, though not necessarily the same form (you may have to add *-s*, *-ed*, or *-ing* at times).

A. 1. The experienced skater ---------------- effortlessly across the ice.

   2. Everyone watched admiringly as the handsome couple ---------------- across the dance floor.

   3. A skilled pianist, she entertained us for hours ---------------- from one song to another without hesitation.

B. 1. He skated so fast that he seemed to ---------------- over the ice.

   2. She ---------------- three books in order to find the answer to one question.

   3. Standing at the edge of the lake, the children ---------------- stones across the water.

C. 1. The bobsled ---------------- to a halt.

   2. After ---------------- all year, the lazy student naturally failed the final exam.

   3. You can save a little gasoline by ---------------- down a long hill.

D. 1. The hockey player ---------------- sideways across the ice.

   2. After the automobile ---------------- to a stop, she realized they were poised at the edge of a steep cliff.

   3. The former professor, who had succumbed to alcoholism, was clearly ---------------- ---------- in the direction of a flophouse on Skid Row.

E. 1. The skier ---------------- triumphantly across the finish line.

   2. After hovering for a moment, the falcon ---------------- down upon its prey.

   3. The mother ---------------- her little girl off the swing and carried her into the house.

IV. After completing Exercise III, try to define the five words by studying the three sentences in which each was used. Give definitions that are as complete as possible. Be sure that your definitions show distinctions that exist among these words.

1. COAST _____

_____

2. GLIDE _____

_____

3. SKID _____

_____

4. SKIM _____

_____

5. SWOOP _____

_____

6
On Target!

Ever since the first primitive man hurled a rock at a twig, humans have been spraining arms and wrenching backs to be "On Target." Some have used arrows, some darts, some horseshoes, and some—with a difference—a foil or a saber.

The sport of Robin Hood and William Tell is the oldest and still one of the most popular.

I. Label the following parts: *arrow, bow, bull's-eye, bowstring, crest, fletching, nock, quiver, shaft, target.*

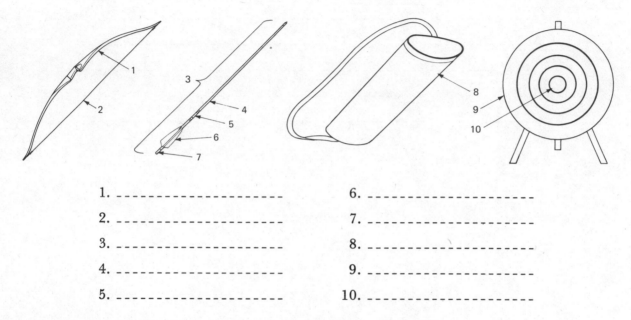

1. _____   6. _____

2. _____   7. _____

3. _____   8. _____

4. _____   9. _____

5. _____   10. _____

II. The target, as you will have noticed, is made up of five circles: the one in the center, the bull's-eye, is gold and is scored at 9 points; the next one is red at 7 points; then blue at 5 points; black at 3 points; and white at 1 point. Below are five multiple-choice statements. Aim for a perfect score—a bull's-eye!

1. To warn other archers on a field range that you are ready to shoot, call _____ ("Timber," "Fore," "Fast").

2. The curve that an arrow makes as it flies through the air is called its _____ _____ (trailer, traction, trajectory).

3. An arrow or a missile that is shot into the air is properly called a _____ (bullet, projectile, probang).

4. After shooting, all archers are expected to *retrieve* their arrows at the same time.

   Retrieve means _____ (wax, recover, exchange).

5. A number of arrows shot simultaneously or in rapid succession is called a _____ (volley, barrage, storm).

Scoring:

One correct answer = 1 point
Two correct answers = 3 points
Three correct answers = 5 points
Four correct answers = 7 points
Five correct answers = 9 points = a bull's-eye!

III. Fencing is not a target sport in the same sense that archery is, but both demand accuracy, strength, and stamina. As fencing becomes more popular, some fencing terms are coming into our daily language. Match the terms in the first column with the definitions in the second.

____	1. foil	*a.* a contest between two individuals
____	2. parry	*b.* a prearranged combat between two persons to settle a point of honor
____	3. engagement	
____	4. bout	*c.* a hit that would puncture or wound if weapons were pointed
____	5. feint	*d.* a hit that would not inflict a puncture or wound
____	6. riposte	*e.* a fencing sword with a thin blade
____	7. duel	*f.* the crossing of blades
____	8. pass	*g.* to ward off a thrust
____	9. touch	*h.* a retaliatory action or movement
____	10. thrust	*i.* to pierce or stab; to push forward forcefully
		j. a movement intended to mislead; a pretended attack

IV. **Analogies**

Complete the following analogies:

1. A round is to archery as a(n) _____ is to fencing.
   (inning, quarter, bout)

2. A bull's-eye is to archery as a _____ is to horseshoes.
   (ringer, grounder, touch)

3. A golf bag is to clubs as a _____ is to arrows.
   (sheath, fletching, quiver)

4. A fist is to a boxer as a _____ is to a fencer.
   (foil, feint, foot)

5. Archery is to a range as skating is to a _____ .
   (pond, rink, sidewalk)

V. To Test Your Deductive Powers

Complete each statement by inserting in each blank one of the words listed below.

crest	projectiles	thrust
duel	retrieve	volley
parried	riposte	

1. They barraged me with a _ of insults.

2. Since I didn't wish to answer him, I _ his questions with a question of my own.

3. As the subway doors started to close, he _ his body between two people in an attempt to get aboard.

4. When snowballs are made with stones inside, they become deadly _ _ _ _ _ _ _ _ _ _ _ _ _ _ _ _ .

5. Determined to _ her purse, she lunged after the pickpocket.

6. H. L. Mencken, whose wit was sharp and biting, had a clever _ for every remark made in his presence.

7. The unfair _ between the courtier and the peasant ended inevitably in the death of the peasant.

8. The _ of an arrow serves to identify the owner of that arrow. In the same way the family _ on silverware serves to identify the owner of that silverware. (same word in both blanks)

7
In the Depths

Although water is an alien element, it holds a subtle and pervasive fascination for many people. Humans traverse it (swimming and boating); they plunge into it (diving); from it they obtain food (fishing) and other valuable substances (pearl diving and coral diving); they play in it (water polo); and they play on it (water skiing and surfing).

In summer heat the ocean lures young and old alike with promises of cool relief. On crisp mornings and on rainy nights it attracts fishermen. In all seasons, by day and by night, it is a Mecca, drawing thousands of pilgrims to work and to play.

It is our *other* home—not so safe as land, but infinitely more mysterious.

I. The root *aqua* means *water*. With this piece of knowledge plus some deductive power, you should be able to match the words in the first column with the definitions in the second.

```
____  1. aquacade      a. board on which one rides as it is towed by a motorboat

____  2. aquaplane     b. related to water, e.g., living in water, occurring in water, etc.

____  3. aquanaut      c. etching that resembles a wash drawing

____  4. aquamarine    d. watery

____  5. aquarium      e. succession of swimming and diving feats for an audience

____  6. aquatic       f. conduit that transports water from one place to another

____  7. aqueduct      g. 11th sign of the zodiac; a constellation

____  8. aqueous       h. someone who works under water doing scientific research

____  9. Aquarius      i. bowl or tank for fish and water plants

____ 10. aquatint      j. light greenish blue
```

II. Now, using a dictionary, try to answer the following "in-depth" questions.

1. Why must a *buoy* be *bouyant*?

   _____

   _____

2. What is the difference between a *nose dive* and a *swan dive*?

   _____

   _____

   _____

3. A *fathom* (used to measure depth of water) equals 6 feet. Why did people years ago describe the ocean as *fathomless*? Why might a profound mind be described as *fathomless*?

   _____

   _____

----

4. SCUBA is an acronym—a word formed from the *initial* or first letters of several words. What are the five words whose initials spell *scuba* and that also define *scuba*?

----

5. *Draft* (or the British *draught*) has many meanings. What does it mean to

a. a sailor _____

b. a hypochondriac _____

c. a young man of military age _____

d. a banker _____

e. a person who has a fireplace in the living room _____

III. To satisfy each definition below in the second column, complete the "water" word in the first column. The number of blanks corresponds to the number of letters missing.

1. water _ _ _ _   *a.* dry; not needing water

2. water- _ _ _   *b.* to "glide" on water while being towed by a boat

3. water _ _ _ _ _ _   *c.* heavy because saturated with water

4. water _ _ _ _ _   *d.* cascade; descending water

5. water _ _ _ _ _ _   *e.* water-soluble paint

6. water _ _ _ _ _ _   *f.* plant used in salads and sandwiches

7. water _ _ _ _ _   *g.* Each of two teams (in the water) tries to pass a ball into the opponent's goal. (2 words)

8. water _ _ _ _ _   *h.* almost invisible design impressed on paper

9. water _ _ _ _ _   *i.* duck or goose or swan

10. water _ _ _ _ _ _   *j.* large fruit, green on the outside, pink on the inside

IV. To Test Your Memory and Your Deductive Powers:

1. If a transparent blue-green gemstone bears the same name as its color, what is it called?

----

2. Diving and swimming are properly called _____ sports.

3. A library houses books; an art museum houses paintings. What would you call a large building that houses exhibits of underwater life? _____

4. Because surfboards are meant to ride lightly over the water, some are filled with plastic foam to provide additional _____ .

5. At depths over 100 feet, or about _____ fathoms, the scuba diver must be on guard against possible nitrogen narcosis.

6. Why are small children generally given watercolors rather than oil paints? _____

   _____

7. List two acronyms in common use and explain the *exact* meaning of each. _____

   _____

8. What is a hypochondriac? _____

   _____

8
Mystery Morsels

1. Why would an astute thief be unlikely to hide a valuable stolen aquamarine in a bowl of strawberries? _____

   _____

2. Maisie wanted to go horseback riding. As she entered the O.K. Stable, she carried a list of equipment that she planned to request. Here is her list:

   bridle   reins   stirrup
   quiver   saddle

   Which piece of equipment would she probably be unable to find and why? _____

   _____

3. Hidden in the paragraph below are five sports. Find them by rearranging the letters in each italicized expression.

   C. F. Ginne jumped out of the *pool*. Without *caring* for appearances, he jumped on his horse and began to *flog* it. Hair *blowing* in the wind, the rider disappeared with his horse behind a mesa.

   _____   _____

   _____   _____

   _____

4. A book thief took three sports mysteries from the local library. Being a considerate fellow, he left a record of the titles and authors. Unfortunately the typewriter he used had no vowels and no spacebar. Can you decode the following titles and authors (last names only) by inserting missing vowels and spaces, and so help the librarian to know what books to reorder?

   a. THTNNSNTMRDR by RCQT

   b. THSKTNGRNKCPR by FRZ

   c. HPHMCD by BSKT

   a. _____

   b. _____

   c. _____

5. What word commonly used in competitive sports means all of the following: (*a*) the written form of a musical selection; (*b*) a grudge; (*c*) a group of 20; (*d*) a numerical record of points made; (*e*) the number grade on an examination.

   Answer: _____

6. By adding the same letter to all of the following words, you can turn them into sports-related terms:

owl	it	oat
out	ounce	all

What is the letter? ____

7. Why would a baseball player like to live in a fast-moving trailer? _____

_____

8. Using rhyme and your knowledge of sports terminology, complete the following verses:

In football, people grumble

If, by chance, you make a _____ .

In bowling, teammates swear

If you only make a _____ .

In archery, you'll rue your plight

If once your arrow hits the _____ .

In diving, this rule on self impose:

Make like a swan, not like a _____ .

In tennis, you'll be called a slob

If more than once you miss a _____ .

In all sports, know, the rules begin:

Play fair, play clean, but *play to win!*

9. Five men have gathered for dinner. They include a carpenter, an ichthyologist, a podiatrist, a potter, and a weaver. Each has a favorite sport. Alphabetically listed the five sports are basketball, bowling, fencing, football, and skating. Interestingly enough, each man's favorite sport is related in some way to his occupation. Figure out which sport is the favorite of each man.

    a. carpenter _____

    b. ichthyologist _____

    c. podiatrist _____

    d. potter _____

    e. weaver _____

10. When is a horseman like a girl on her wedding day? _____

_____

11. What woman separates basketball from baseball? _____

Seven. Words to Travel By

1
A Concrete Nation

"Autobat," "ipsometer," "trundler," "autogen," and "molectro" were among the names suggested for the new self-propelled vehicles that were beginning to appear on the roads in the early years of this century. For a long time the French Academy, a rather solemn and pedantic assembly, struggled with this question. Then it carefully constructed a highly appropriate term from two word elements: *auto* (meaning "self") and *mobile* (meaning "moving"). So *automobile* came into existence—a fine example of a word deliberately coined to name something that had not existed before.

I. A. The two parts of the word *automobile* are also parts of many other words. Try to answer the following questions by remembering the meaning of *auto* and by noting the context.

1. Because Helen Keller herself wrote *The Story of My Life*, the book is classified as an *autobiography*. What is an *auto*biography? _

_ _

2. Fans often ask Chris Evert for her *autograph*. What is an *auto*graph? _ _ _ _ _ _ _ _ _ _ _

_ _

3. Some communes, rebelling against the established government, are striving to become *autonomous*. What kind of government do these people want? _ _ _ _ _ _ _ _ _

_ _

4. Some psychologists believe that certain fears are the result of *autosuggestion*. How do such fears come into being? _

_ _

5. The *autistic* child is one who has withdrawn from reality. *To* what has he withdrawn? _

_ _

B. Now try the same technique with these *mobile* words:

1. In the last few decades Americans have become increasingly *mobile*. This has resulted in new problems based on rootlessness. What does *mobile* mean in the first sentence? _

_ _

2. Tennis and basketball both demand *mobility* for success. What physical aptitude do

these sports demand? _____

3. Within the last few years more and more people are investing in *mobile* homes. What is a *mobile* home? _____

4. A fairly new kind of sculpture, usually with many parts, is the *mobile*. What do the parts probably do? _____ Have you ever seen a *mobile*? _____ If so, describe it. _____

_____

5. When criminals increase their activity, police commissioners often respond by *mobilizing* their departments. What does *mobilize* mean? _____

_____

II. Nondrivers, as well as drivers, should know the abbreviations and symbols that are commonly used on maps, on the road, and in descriptions of a car's operation. How many of the following abbreviations and symbols can you identify?

1. rte. _____

2. mph _____

3. r.p.m. _____

4. rd. _____

5. tpk. _____

6. **20** _____

7. **86** _____

8. gal. _____

9. ⬡ _____

10. hp _____

III. **Psyching the Manufacturer**

Whenever a manufacturer names a new model, he keeps the customer's desires in mind. For example, if he calls a car a Mustang, he is appealing to the would-be cowboy type who likes to see himself in control of a spirited horse. Below are the names of 10 popular car models. After each name, write the meaning of the name and the probable appeal the manufacturer had in mind.

1. Valiant _____

_____

2. Cutlass _____

_____

3. Matador _____

_____

4. Maverick _____

_____

5. Gremlin _____

    _____

6. Hornet _____

    _____

7. Riviera _____

    _____

8. Caprice _____

    _____

9. Barracuda _____

    _____

10. Comet _____

    _____

IV. Car Catechism

Using a dictionary and some common sense, see how many of the following questions you can answer.

1. What is meant by *highway hypnosis*? _____

    _____

2. What is meant by *vehicular homicide*? _____

    _____

3. What is a *hairpin turn*? _____

    _____

4. There are *defensive* plays in football, *defensive* moves in chess, and *defensive* driving. What is *defensive* driving? _____

    _____

5. When you buy a car, you will discover that some equipment is *optional*. What does this mean? _____

    Name one piece of *optional* equipment. _____

6. There are *contour* maps, *contour* farming, and now *contour* seats. How do *contour* seats differ from traditional automobile seats? _____

    _____

7. You may not wear a *muffler* around your neck, but you must have a *muffler* on your car. What is each kind of *muffler* designed to do? _____

    _____

----

8. *Smog*, a result of air pollution, is a blend, that is, a word formed by combining two other words. Which two words, blended, form *smog*? ------------------------

9. Most roads have a posted *maximum* speed. Some roads also have a posted *minimum* speed. Why are both necessary on the new superhighways? ----------------------

----

----

10. Name three physical conditions that make driving *hazardous*. --------------------

----

2
On a Bicycle Built for . . .

What vehicle can be used by people of all ages, causes no pollution, and comes with one wheel, two wheels, or three wheels?
Answer: the unicycle-bicycle-tricycle, of course!

I. Cycle wheels, whether they come singly, doubly, or triply, always have spokes. Provide spokes for the three wheels below by starting with the prefix at the hub and adding the letters needed to satisfy each of the definitions below each wheel.

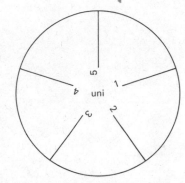 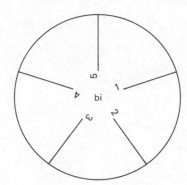 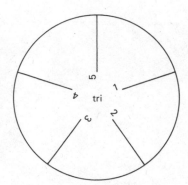

1. to bring together into one	1. eyeglasses with two kinds of lenses	1. three people performing together
2. outfit worn by all people doing the same kind of work	2. able to speak two languages	2. three-legged stand used to hold a camera
3. legendary animal with the body and head of a horse and one horn	3. supported by members of two political parties	3. three-sided figure
4. one-sided	4. to cut into two equal parts	4. long three-pronged fork often associated with the sea
5. exact agreement	5. involving the use of the two eyes at the same time	5. three related literary works

II. Five parts of a bicycle are the *brake*, the *handlebar*, the *hub* of the wheel, the *pedal*, and the *saddle*. Label each of these parts on the sketch on the next page.

Now link each of the above five words with one of the definitions below:

6. a center of activity _ _ _ _ _ _ _ _ _ _ _ _ _ _ _ _ _

7. a foot lever on a piano _ _ _ _ _ _ _ _ _ _ _ _ _ _ _ _

8. describing a long, curved mustache _ _ _ _ _ _ _ _ _ _ _ _ _ _ _ _ _

9. a depression in the ridge of a hill _ _ _ _ _ _ _ _ _ _ _ _ _ _ _ _ _

10. a thicket; an area with heavy undergrowth _ _ _ _ _ _ _ _ _ _ _ _ _ _ _ _

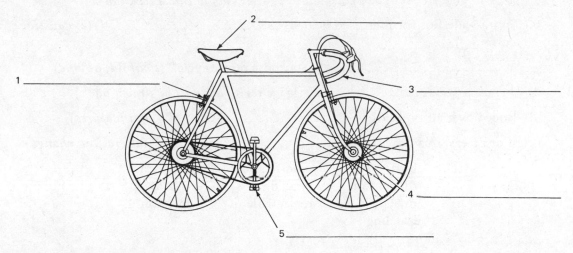

III. Describing a Bicycle

See if you can find in the list below the adjectives needed to complete sentences 1–5 correctly.

custom-built   maneuverable   versatile

elegant   sturdy

1. If a bicycle is graceful, attractive, symmetrical, and costly, it may be described as _ _ _ _

   _ .

2. If a bicycle is built substantially, it may be described as _ .

3. If a bicycle can be easily steered and if it responds quickly to change of direction, it

   may be described as _ .

4. If a bicycle is efficient on long *and* short rides, on concrete *and* on dirt roads, and is

   dependable *and* attractive, it may be described as _ .

5. If a bicycle is made for a particular person in accordance with that person's specifica-

   tions, it may be described as _ .

IV. Motorcycles

Below are 10 quotations taken from a typical issue of *Cycle World*, a magazine for motorcyclists. Each quotation has a word missing; next to each quotation is the definition of the missing word. Below the 10 quotations is a list of the 10 missing words. Try to complete each quotation correctly.

1. "through some _ trail" (*severely punishing*)

2. "this model has been _ out" (*eliminated one step at a time*)

3. "the _ point at 6,000 r.p.m." (*the condition of moving back and forth rapidly*)

4. " _ speeds of 110 mph" (*continued; maintained*)

5. "every cycle _ " (*an enthusiast; a fan*)

6. "extra-wide fins for increased heat _ " (*exhaustion; scattering*)

7. "a _ -purpose motorcycle" (*twofold; double*)

8. "_ luggage rack" (*able to be drawn back*)

9. "speed over all types of _ " (*land features*)

10. "For racers, this _ is a must." (*alteration; change*)

buff	modification	sustained
dissipation	phased	terrain
dual	retractable	vibration
grueling		

3
The Roller Derby

If the person who invented the wheel were still around and receiving royalties, he (or she!) would make Howard Hughes look like a pauper! For the ubiquitous wheel is, both literally and metaphorically, what makes the modern world go round.

I. Search your memory and prod your imagination and see if you can name 20 "things" that are equipped with *wheels*. (*Clue*: Don't forget ordinary household appliances as well as the various kinds of vehicles.)

1. _____ 11. _____
2. _____ 12. _____
3. _____ 13. _____
4. _____ 14. _____
5. _____ 15. _____
6. _____ 16. _____
7. _____ 17. _____
8. _____ 18. _____
9. _____ 19. _____
10. _____ 20. _____

II. Surely among your 20 selections you included *roller skates*. People have been skating for a long time, but with the coming of television, the Roller Derby came into its own. Here are 10 sentences that could be used in describing a Roller Derby and its participants. After each one, define the italicized word or phrase.

1. The Roller Derby is considered a *contact sport*. _____
_____

2. The first thing a contestant must learn is to keep his *equilibrium* even when he is being shoved and elbowed. _____

3. Spectators observed the *circling pack* with keen interest. _____
_____

4. After the completion of one *lap*, a few contestants drew away from the pack. _____
_____

5. As the Derby continued, the *arena* rocked with shouts, boos, and unrestrained high spirits. _____
_____

6. A *jam* is hazardous for the contestants and thrilling for the spectators. ------------

----

7. The result of many jams is a few real and many *feigned* injuries. ------------------

8. Even more exciting to spectators are the rough-and-tumble *melees* that are part of almost every Derby. --

9. It has been said that experienced entries are as skilled in crowd-pleasing *theatrics* as they are in skating. --

10. Because the Derby is held in cities across the continent, most skaters quickly develop a *nomadic* life style. --

III. Certain adjectives appear regularly in stories describing Roller Derbies. Match the italicized adjectives in the first column with the definitions in the second.

---- 1. *exotic* stunt   *a.* threefold

---- 2. *flailing* arms   *b.* built with a slope toward the outer edge

---- 3. *flawless* performance   *c.* energetic; lively

---- 4. *dramatic* flair   *d.* unusual; strange and therefore striking

---- 5. *triple* twist   *e.* showy; very elaborate; vivid

---- 6. *fluid* motion   *f.* having emotional appeal; forceful

---- 7. *flamboyant* poses   *g.* waving; swinging

---- 8. *banked* track   *h.* increased; stepped-up

---- 9. *accelerated* motion   *i.* smooth; effortless

---- 10. *vigorous* gestures   *j.* perfect; without error

IV. Here are a few exercises pertaining to wheels:

A. What kind of wheel is used

1. to maneuver a car? ------------------------------

2. to make yarn or thread? ------------------------------

3. to shape a bowl or vase? ------------------------------

4. to turn running water into power? ------------------------------

5. to propel a boat? ------------------------------

B. What "wheel" words are defined below?

1. a movable seat used by the disabled ------------------------------

2. a vehicle with handles used to move materials ------------------------------

3. the distance from the rear axle to the front axle in a car _____

4. a person with a great deal of power (2 words; slang) _____

5. a sharp operator; a shrewd bargainer (slang) _____

6. a handspring made with arms and legs spread apart _____

7. a toy made with plastic vanes that spin when blown _____

8. an extra person (e.g., at a party) _____

9. operating without heeding rules _____

4
The Lonely Whistle

Planes are faster and automobiles more convenient, but no vehicle has more of a grip on the imagination and dreams of the American people than the railroad train. Hundreds of mystery stories have used trains as their setting: criminals strike, then—as the train slows down—slip quietly off the train into the darkness. Millionaires occasionally still rent an entire train to convey themselves and their friends to some far-off oasis of pleasure. Children, wide-eyed and expectant, stand at stations hoping to see the engine round the bend and pull up, shuddering, to a stop. Above all, people of all ages listen in a special way to the lonely, alluring whistle of the train traveling through the night. In a practical sense, trains may be less important than they used to be; in an inspirational sense, they are just as important as ever.

I. The *locomotive* (a self-propelled engine) is the heart of the train. Whether it operates by steam or by electricity, it pulls the other cars behind it. Some of the most common cars are the *boxcar*, the *caboose*, the *flatcar*, the *observation car*, and the *tank car*. Using common sense (and the process of elimination), try to connect each of the five cars above with one of the descriptions below.

1. _____ a car of a freight train for the use of the train crew and railroad workmen

2. _____ car often equipped with a glass or plastic dome to permit viewing of scenery

3. _____ enclosed car used for transportation of freight

4. _____ car equipped with tanks used to transport oil or other liquids

5. _____ freight car without sides or top

II. Passengers who wish to travel by train will find various kinds of accommodations. Some types require reservations, and to handle these the larger railroads have installed computerized reservation systems. You might, for example, choose to travel by *coach*, by *compartment*, by *parlor car*, by *pullman*, or by *roomette*. Match each with its appropriate description.

1. _____ sleeping car with upper and lower berths

2. _____ ordinary passenger car (not reserved)

3. _____ small private room (for one person) for sitting and sleeping

4. _____ slightly larger private room (for two people) for sitting and sleeping

5. _____ car with individual reserved seats. Seats are usually larger and more comfortable.

III. Trains form a major part of any *transit* (public transportation) system. They are especially useful for *mass* transit. Most trains provide both *local* service (stops at every station) and *express service* (stops at large stations only). Present railway systems include *Amtrak*, *elevated railroads*, *Metroliners*, *monorails*, and *subways*. Match each kind of system with its definition.

1. _____ underground railroad systems

2. _____ trains traveling on a single rail

3. _____ reorganization of trains intended to provide fast, efficient service

4. _____ trains providing fast service between New York and Washington, D.C.

5. _____ railways operating on a raised structure

IV. A good many terms are necessary to describe the operation of a railroad. Some of them are technical and need to be known only by railroad personnel, but others should be known by everyone. Match the railroad terms in the first column with the definitions in the second column.

____ 1. cowcatcher   *a.* device used to transfer cars from one track to another

____ 2. trestle   *b.* condition of running off the tracks

____ 3. whistle-stop   *c.* short sidetrack branching out from the main track

____ 4. spur   *d.* iron frame in front of a locomotive once needed to sweep cattle off the tracks

____ 5. switch

____ 6. roundhouse   *e.* place visited briefly in the middle of a longer trip

____ 7. railroad tie   *f.* station at the end of a railroad line

____ 8. terminal   *g.* a framework of timbers or steel used to support a bridge

____ 9. derailment   *h.* circular building used to house and switch locomotives

____ 10. stopover   *i.* a town, usually small, at which trains stop only when signaled

                            j. one of the timbers across a railroad bed used to support the tracks

V. Various kinds of people are needed to operate railroads. Define the job of each of the people listed below:

1. brakeman: _____

_____

2. conductor: _____

_____

3. dispatcher: _____

_____

4. engineer: _____

_____

5. station master: _____

_____

VI. To Test Your Deductive Powers

1. A *tycoon* is a businessman who has made a great deal of money. What is a *railroad tycoon*? _____

_____

2. Why is a locomotive sometimes called an *iron horse*? _____

_____

3. You know what a locomotive looks like. Why might an engine be described as *mammoth*? _____

_____

4. Remembering the meaning of railroad *terminal*, what do you think is meant by the term *terminal illness*? _____

_____

5. If, when you leave the classroom to go to the library, your teacher tells you to travel *express*, what is she clearly suggesting? _____

_____

5

The Wild Blue Yonder

One of the smartest things a human being can do is to learn to use knowledge he already has to create knowledge he would like to acquire. Here's a short "plane program" that should help you to do just that.

I. Consider the phrase *automatic pilot*. You know what a *pilot* is, and you probably know what *automatic* means (certainly you know that the prefix *auto* means "self"). Therefore, you can deduce that if a plane is equipped with automatic pilot, it can literally (1)

_____ . Since *autopilot* and *robot pilot* mean the same, you also know these two terms.

Air forces are seldom *autonomous*; they usually operate under the supervision and policies of a government. But in 1921 the Italian Air Force, in an attempt to increase efficiency, became *autonomous*. Autonomous must mean (2) _____

_____ .

You also know that the prefix "super" means "greater than" or "superior to"; so you know that a *superjet* is merely a (3) _____ .
If you also know that "sonic" relates to the speed of sound in air (about 738 miles per hour at sea level), then you know that a supersonic jet is capable of traveling at speeds greater than (4) _____ .

The prefix "anti" means "against," as you probably know from antifreeze and anti-social. The word *antiaircraft*, therefore, would necessarily refer to something (5) _____

_____ , while the term *antimissile missile* would refer to (6) _____

_____

_____ .

An *aerial* is another name for a television or radio antenna—something that permits the sending and receiving of messages *through the air*. *Aerial* simply describes something *in* the air or *of* the air or related *to* the air. A bird may be described as an *aerial* creature because it (7) _____ . A view from the air (from an airplane, for example) is called an (8) _____ . If one nation wants *aerial supremacy*, it wants (9) _____ .
Combine the meaning of *aer* and *naut* (sailor), and you know that *aeronautics* is the theory and practice of (10) _____ .

Sometimes it helps to look at words in pairs. Consider the meaning of *domestic* and *international*. Then decide—what is the difference between *domestic* air traffic and *international* air traffic? (11) _____

_____ (12) _____

_____

In football the team on the *offensive* wants to gain possession of the ball and take it into enemy territory. The team on the *defensive* wants to protect the ball and/or its territory. Therefore, a fighter plane that is designed to protect a country from invading bombers is primarily (13) _____ aircraft, while the bomber itself is (14) _____ aircraft.

You have probably used the slang term "flak," meaning excessive criticism. You may, for example, have complained about "flak" from parents and teachers when you are neglecting your studies. In the original sense does "flak" refer to bursting shells or to aircraft maneuvers? (15) _____

II. Use present knowledge, deduction, and the process of elimination to match the italicized words in the first column with the definitions in the second.

____ 1. *operational* airfield	a.	planes making short, frequent trips between two points
____ 2. *tarmac*	b.	upside down; in a reversed position
____ 3. boarding *ramp*	c.	working; functioning properly
____ 4. air *parity*	d.	equality in power or amount
____ 5. *hangar*	e.	electronic determination of the distance of far-off objects
____ 6. *inverted* flying		
____ 7. *cruising* at 600 mph	f.	traveling at sustained even speed
____ 8. bomber *formation*	g.	sloping passage
____ 9. *shuttles*	h.	shed for housing airplanes
____ 10. *radar*	i.	area paved with crushed stone and tar binder
	j.	preplanned arrangement; flying order

III. Here are five aircraft-related words:

blitzkrieg   obsolescence   squadron
maneuverability   range

Complete each of the following sentences by inserting one of these words in each blank:

1. Before stopping for refueling or other maintenance, the small plane had a maximum _____ of 300 miles.

2. In World War II more than one European city was a victim of the _____ _____ , an offensive by the German Army and Air Force.

3. He was loyal to his _____ and to the larger group of which it was a part.

4. New planes are being designed and manufactured so rapidly that within a couple of years a plane can be scrapped because of _____ .

5. The _____ of the plane permitted the pilot to swoop between two skyscrapers, climb over an unexpected mountain, and avoid a flock of birds that emerged suddenly from the clouds.

IV. To Test Your Deductive Powers

1. If only the second of three vending machines is still *operational*, how does it differ from the other two? _____

2. If the first-grade class suddenly decides it wishes to be *autonomous*, why might the teacher, principal, and parents be worried? _____
   _____

3. If a small car has greater *maneuverability* while a large car has greater power, why would the small car be more useful in dense city traffic? _____
   _____

4. Why do many of the superhighways use entrance and exit *ramps*? _____
   _____

5. What is planned *obsolescence*? _____
   _____
   How has planned obsolescence helped to bring us to the present ecological crisis?
   _____
   _____

6
Mongrel Mysteries

A *mongrel* dog is one that is the product of the mixing of breeds. Here are a few mongrel mysteries for you to solve.

1. Hasty Hannah, the star of the Roller Derby, was scheduled to appear on the local television quiz show. Unfortunately, three women showed up, not one. Each had red hair, each was wearing roller skates, and each claimed to be Hasty Hannah. The master of ceremonies had one minute to find out which one was the real Hasty Hannah. He asked all of them to write down the answers to three questions: (1) What is a *banked track*? (2) What is a *jam*?, and (3) What is a *lap*? Here are their answers:

   Hannah #1: (1) A banked track is a track that has been financed by the bank.
   　　　　　　 (2) A jam occurs when a skater's wheels lock.
   　　　　　　 (3) A lap is a measured mile.

   Hannah #2: (1) A banked track is a track built with a slope toward the outer edge.
   　　　　　　 (2) A jam occurs when many skaters congest in one area.
   　　　　　　 (3) A lap is one circuit of a track.

   Hannah #3: (1) A banked track is a track lined with guard rails or low cement walls.
   　　　　　　 (2) A jam occurs when one skater collides with another.
   　　　　　　 (3) A lap is the last stretch of the track, usually one-quarter of a mile.

   As soon as the M.C. read the answers, he singled out the real Hasty Hannah and had the two imposters arrested for false impersonation. Which was the real Hasty Hannah—#1, 2, or 3? How was the M.C. able to spot the two imposters?

   ----

2. Four strangers met on the Appalachian Trail. After supper on the first night, they sat around the fire and swapped stories about their jobs. The first claimed that he was a railroad man, and he spoke knowledgeably about cabooses and trestles and cowcatchers. The second stated that he was an automobile salesman, and he knew all about contour seats, mufflers, and optional equipment. The third said he designed motorcyles, and he talked about retractable luggage racks, roundhouses, and vibration points. The fourth declared that he was a pilot, and he discussed boarding ramps, hangars, and maximum flying range.

   At midnight one of them turned on a transistor radio. "An escaped convict is in the area," warned the newscaster. "He is believed to be dangerous. He can be identified by the lies he tells about his line of work."

   The four men looked at each other and reviewed the stories they had exchanged. Suddenly three of them jumped the fourth, and wrestled him to the ground. While two of them held him down, the third went to the police. Who was the escaped convict? What mistake did he make that told the others that he had lied about his line of work?

   ----

3. "You can't hold me responsible, Your Honor," said Big Jeb in a loud voice. "It wasn't my fault. It was highway hypnosis. You read about it happening all the time. I didn't see my brother when he stepped into the road. I was kinda in a trance—that highway hypnosis thing, you know. I just hit him and killed him. But it wasn't my fault! All the books will tell you."

The judge looked solemn. "Where did this happen, Jeb?"

Big Jeb thought for a minute, then explained. "I'd just pulled out of the garage, and I was going down the driveway. We have a pretty long driveway, Your Honor—about 100 feet, and it's not in very good condition. I have to admit that. It's bumpy and there are weeds, and there are even a couple of potholes. But my brother Dirk—well, he just stepped out in front of me, and with that highway hypnosis thing, I just naturally ran into him. I couldn't help it."

Why did the Judge have Jeb booked for homicide?

Eight. Words for Tomorrow

1

A Medley of Monsters

Atop the Cathedral of Notre Dame is a collection of gargoyles: rainspouts that resemble monsters, half-human, half-animal. Here is one at the right:

Notice the simian (apelike) face, the single, thick horn protruding from the head, the thin, ugly wings, the human hands. It is grotesque in the same way evil is grotesque: frightening in its distortion, yet ludicrous, too.

Think of a more modern example: Grinch, the animated cartoon villain. Grinch is a kind of mobile gargoyle. We shudder while we laugh.

The quality of the grotesque is shared by just about every monster ever conceived by the human brain.

I. Monsters are *mythical* creatures, that is, they are legendary. They never really existed; they don't exist now. But every age has terrified itself with monster stories. Here are 12 notorious monsters. Try to match each with its description.

---- 1. basilisk
---- 2. griffin
---- 3. roc
---- 4. centaur
---- 5. chimera
---- 6. sphinx
---- 7. kraken
---- 8. dragon
---- 9. mermaid
---- 10. abominable snowman
---- 11. frankenstein
---- 12. harpy

a. giant reptile; claws of a lion, tail of a serpent, wings, scaly skin

b. hirsute (hairy) manlike creature seen in the Himalayas; also called "yeti"

c. head of a lion, body of a goat, tail of a serpent; breathes fire

d. dragon or serpent whose breath or look is deadly

e. bird of enormous size and strength

f. head and wings of an eagle; body of a lion

g. head and upper body of a woman; tail of a fish

h. woman's head and bird's body; wings and talons

i. monster that looks like a human and that destroys its creator

j. head and upper body of a man; lower body of a horse

k. sea monster (probably giant squid); usually found in Norwegian waters

l. body of a lion, head of a man; sometimes winged

II. As you may know, monsters come in three general types: some prefer the water, some roam the land, and some come from outer space. Those that prefer the water are *aquatic* monsters like the sea serpent and the kraken; those that roam the land are *terrestrial* monsters like the abominable snowman; those that come from outer space are *extraterrestrial* monsters like the little green Martians we occasionally hear about. All would lose their power instantly if people were not *superstitious*. All are—or have been—*controversial*, the subject of many arguments. One or another of them has occasionally been the subject of a *hoax*, as when a photographer fakes a picture. And for almost every monster there is a monster *buff*—a sort of modified fanatic whose imagination is excited by monsters and everything about them.

III. The monster buff has a terminology of his own. Here are 15 adjectives that are frequently used to describe monsters. If you can match each adjective with its definition, you will be ready to enter the Monster Marathon.

bizarre	fierce	potent
colossal	lethal	preposterous
diabolical	macabre	repulsive
extravagant	malodorous	serpentine
fabulous	maniacal	sinister

1. tremendous; stupendous _____
2. ferocious; savage _____
3. mad; crazed; frenzied _____
4. gruesome; horrible _____
5. evil; ominous _____
6. farfetched; unconventional; odd _____
7. astounding; astonishing _____
8. winding; sinuous; sly _____
9. disgusting _____
10. lavish; unrestrained _____
11. ill-smelling _____
12. contrary to common sense or reason _____
13. capable of causing death _____
14. very strong; powerful _____
15. devilish; satanic _____

IV. In the Middle Ages people enjoyed reading stories about animals—and sometimes monsters—that ended with a moral. Collections of these stories were called *bestiaries*, and they were often elaborately illustrated. Make up your own monster, and write a short story about it that teaches a moral.

V. To Test Your Memory and Your Deductive Powers

How many of the following sentences can you complete correctly? Use the words in the list below.

aquatic	extraterrestrial	lethal
bestiary	frankenstein	mythical
bizarre	harpy	sinister
colossus		

1. Her hat, a fantastic creation of feathers, straw, and ribbon, is—to put it mildly—_ .

2. Having grown up on the shore of the Atlantic Ocean, he was skilled in most of the _ sports.

3. The new statue of Columbus in the park is so enormous that it has been nicknamed the "_ of Oakville."

4. Miss Catkins, the shrewish woman who fluttered around during the party like a bird of prey, is our neighborhood _ .

5. Both parents had so rigidly disciplined their son that when he turned on them in fury, they realized they had created a _ .

6. A book of stories that teaches morality through the use of animal characters is called a _ .

7. As we thrashed helplessly in the water, his boat was the only one in sight; but his _ smile warned us at once that we could expect no help from him.

8. No monster has yet been proved real; all are _ .

9. The flying saucers that have been "seen" in the sky during the last three decades are often believed to be _ machines.

10. A gun or a knife, like the stare of a basilisk, may be _ .

2
Earth to Mars

Space Age: the period of time beginning with the launching of the first man-made satellite to orbit around the earth. That first satellite was Sputnik I, a Russian vehicle, sent up on October 4, 1957. The Space Age has not yet reached its majority, and already special Space Age dictionaries are available. Not since the Renaissance have so many new words exploded with such intensity into our current language.

I. You know what a space vehicle is, and a space suit, and a space laboratory. But do you know that *space law* is being developed because international rules are needed to govern the use of space? And that *space medicine* is a growing field as doctors try to prevent, diagnose, and cure illnesses resulting from space travel?

Below are a few space-related words that practically everyone knows. Can you define each of them without consulting a dictionary?

1. orbit _____

2. launching pad _____

3. countdown _____

4. backpack _____

5. blast-off _____

Item #1: Did you know that a *bubble colony* is a name for something that doesn't yet exist—for an artificially created Earth environment that can be placed on the moon?

II. Expand your knowledge by explaining the difference between the two expressions in each of the following pairs:

1. *astronaut* and *cosmonaut* _____

_____

_____

2. *offensive missile* and *defensive missile* _____

_____

_____

3. *optical tracking* and *radio tracking* _____

_____

_____

4. *acceleration* and *deceleration* _____

_____

_____

5. *air-to-surface missile* and *surface-to-air missile* _____

_____

_____

Item #2: Did you know that an antimissile missile is jokingly called an *"auntie"*?

III. Now try to match the words in the first column with the definitions in the second:

---- 1. blip   *a.* return of a spacecraft into the earth's atmosphere

---- 2. drift   *b.* landing of space capsule in water rather than on land

---- 3. dry run   *c.* source of power for a rocket engine

---- 4. splashdown   *d.* streak of light on a radar screen indicating the appearance of a machine or some other object in the area being studied

---- 5. simulation

---- 6. velocity   *e.* trial countdown to test readiness of rocket for launching

---- 7. re-entry   *f.* cargo a rocket is carrying

---- 8. pay load   *g.* imitation; artificial visual projection

---- 9. propellant   *h.* transfer of microbes from Earth to another planet, or from another planet to Earth

---- 10. contamination

i. sideways motion of a vehicle as a result of side winds

j. speed an object travels in a particular direction

Item #3: Did you know that a rocket is sometimes called a *bird* and sometimes a *beast*?

IV. An *acronym* is a word formed by combining the first letters or syllables of several words. (CORE, for example, comes from *C*ongress *o*f *R*acial *E*quality.) The Space Age has led to the creation of a whole new group of acronyms. Here are 10 recently developed acronyms. Link each with one of the defining phrases.

BOSS   PET   RAT
laser   RACE   SAM
LEM   radar   SMART
MODS

1. radio detecting and ranging _____

2. surface-to-air missile _____

3. bioastronautical orbiting space station _____

4. production environmental testing _____

5. light amplification by stimulated emission of radiation _____

6. lunar excursion module _____

7. rapid automatic checkout equipment _____

8. manned orbital development station _____

9. supersonic military aircraft research track _____

10. rocket-assisted torpedo _____

Item #4: Did you know that a *light year* (the distance light travels in one year) is about 6 trillion miles?

V. Moon Business

If you hope to visit the moon someday, you will want to know the following terms: *crater*, *rill*, *moon crawler*, *lunar satellite*, *lunar base*.

1. A space vehicle that orbits the moon is a _____ .

2. A pit, or cavity, on the surface of the moon is a _____ .

3. A projected installation on the moon that would be useful for traveling to more distant planets is a _____ .

4. A vehicle with caterpillar treads for traveling over lunar terrain is a _____ .

5. A long, narrow valley on the moon's surface is a _____ .

Item #5: Did you know that the word *galaxy* denotes the stars in our Milky Way—those closest to the Earth—and that *extragalactic* refers to star systems that lie *beyond* our stars?

VI. To Test Your Deductive Powers

1. Why was the name *Gemini* given to the space capsule designed for two men? _____

_____

_____

2. Why was the spacecraft equipped with television cameras to explore the moon's surface called the *Surveyor*? _____

_____

_____

3. Why is the communications satellite that reflects radio signals called the *Echo*? _____

_____

_____

4. Why was the surface-to-air missile that was designed to attack low-flying planes called a

Hawk? ---

----

5. Why were some of the earliest long-distance space probes called the *Pioneers*? -------

----

3
Life in the Year 2000

Where do we go from here?

We have automobiles and airplanes and heart transplants; space capsules and satellites; nuclear energy and miracle drugs and freeze-dried foods. Where do we go from here?

Even now scientists are drawing up *estimates* (tentative judgments) and, with the help of computers, arriving at *projections* (suppositions about future possibilities). With these as a starting point, we can come up with all kinds of marvelous "looks into the future."

I. One of the most important aids in any look into the future is the computer. A computer is simply an electronic machine that can process and store information and later use this information in different ways. It can develop plans of action, correlate thousands of details, even build wholly new conclusions to complex problems. Most computer language is for the specialist, but the average person should know a few of the more popular terms. Here are five of them.

> data processing   print-out
> information retrieval   simulation
> input

Combine common sense and word sense to figure out how to place each of the above words into one of the sentences below.

1. The information actually "fed" into a computer is called the _____

_____ .

2. A visual representation of an object's functioning, a(n) _____

_____ , can be created by a computer. Even before we *saw* our first vehicle land on the moon, with the aid of this process we knew exactly how it would land and how it would look as it landed.

3. When someone prepares information to be used by a computer *or* has a computer

organize the information in a particular way, that person is said to be involved in

_____ .

4. _____ occurs when a computer is asked to bring forth information that had been fed into it at an earlier time.

5. The _____ of a computer is the visible end-product: the organization of information, or the results drawn by the computer from the information fed into it.

II. Drawing distinctions between two related expressions can help to establish meanings clearly. You may need to consult a dictionary to explain how the two expressions in each of the following pairs differ.

1. You all know what a *metropolis* is, but by the year 2000 you will probably be more

concerned with a *megalopolis*. How do they differ? _____

----

2. Scientists are already able to develop and control a *microclimate;* by the year 2000 they

may well be able to control the *macroclimate* too. What do the two words mean?

----

3. Right now we are familiar with a *donor-heart*, but increasingly popular are the *culture-*

grown heart and the *artificial heart*. What exactly is each? --------------------

----

----

4. Your present TV is *two-dimensional*, but some technicians believe that a life-size *three-*

dimensional picture will soon be a reality. How would the three-dimensional picture

differ from the two-dimensional picture? ------------------------------------

----

III. Even your own home will be different in the year 2000. Insert definitions for the italicized
words. Then answer the related questions.

1. The lights in your home may be *actuated* (------------------------------) by

sensors (--

------------------). Can you think of one problem this might create? ---------

----

----

2. The house itself may well have been *prefabricated* (----------------------------

------------------------), which probably means that you can add a *module* (----

------------------------) at will. What is today's equivalent of a module? -----

---------------------------------- Why will it be easier to add one in 2000

than it would be now? --

----

3. By 2000 your house may be *solar-heated* (----------------------------------).

Roofs and walls will be tilted and surfaced to *absorb* (-----------------) or *reflect*

(---------------------) sun and heat, depending on the season. During which

season would you want your house to absorb the sun's heat? ------------ During

which season would you want your house to reflect the sun's heat? ------------

4. It is just possible that by 2000 every house will have a *robot* (---------------------

--) to take
care of cleaning and general maintenance. Would you prefer that your robot look like
a machine or a human being? ----------------------------- Why? -------------

----

5. You may not like the idea of living in a glass-walled house, but would it make a
   difference if you could press a button and make the glass walls *opaque* (-----------
   --) when you desired?
   ------- Why? ---

IV. Many intriguing processes *may* be in existence in the year 2000. Some have already
    appeared, while others are as yet only concepts. How up-to-date are you? Can you match
    the processes in the first column with the definitions in the second?

---- 1. desalination	*a.* desk with three walls, sometimes wired, used for reading, viewing, etc.
---- 2. ESP	*b.* preserving bodies in extremely low temperatures
---- 3. freeze-drying	
---- 4. cybernation	*c.* preserving foods by freezing them rapidly, then drying them in a vacuum
---- 5. speech compression	*d.* the removal of salt from water
---- 6. learning box	*e.* the use of dry ice crystals to stimulate rainfall
---- 7. study carrel	*f.* electronic graph showing characteristics of an individual's speech
---- 8. voiceprint	
---- 9. hypothermia	*g.* perception (the act of knowing something) by methods going beyond the ordinary senses
---- 10. cloud seeding	*h.* automatic control by a computer
	i. machine that enables a student to learn at his own rate, with minimum chance of failure
	j. technique for recording voices at high speed and for permitting listening at high speed

4

The Age of Superman

Would you like to be immortal—to live forever? Would you like to be smarter than you are? Would you like, in a few years, to choose to have a daughter rather than a son? A child with blue eyes rather than with brown? Would you like to go to sleep and wake up 1,000 years from now? Would you like to go to a body shop not for a new fender or a new headlight but for a new eye (because yours is growing weak) or for a new set of fingers (because yours won't quite reach a full octave on the piano)? In short, would you like to be the Clark Kent of tomorrow—the new Superman?

The Age of Superman is just around the corner. Amazing things have happened medically in the last 25 years, and it is probable that still more amazing things will happen in the next 25. You are doubtless familiar with some of the new terminology; you should be familiar with most of it. Why? Because in a couple of decades, *your* generation may have to make some strange and incredibly difficult moral decisions.

I. Quest for Immortality

For example, extensive *prolongation* of life is becoming possible. Some people with weak hearts have *pacemakers* implanted; these are electronic gadgets that *pace* the heart and keep it beating at the proper tempo. Some people receive kidney *transplants* or heart *transplants* from donors. Almost everyone hopes for *longevity*—to live a long time. If modern medicine prolongs life for millions of people, will the world soon be overpopulated? Will there be an enormous *geriatrics* problem as more and more older people live on?

Now choose one of the italicized words in the paragraph above to complete each of the following sentences.

1. If you take an organ from one person and place it in another, the result is a _ _ _ _ _ _ _ _ _

   _ _ _ _ _ _ _ _ _ _ _ _ _ _ _ .

2. To control the rhythm of operation of the heart, one sometimes needs a _ _ _ _ _ _ _ _ _ _ _

   _ _ _ _ _ _ _ _ _ _ _ _ _.

3. A study of the medical problems related to old age is called _ .

4. Some families are known for their _ ; they live to be 80, 90, even 100 years old.

5. Not heeding a doctor's orders is one way of bringing about a _ _ _ _ _ _ _ _ _ _ _ _ _ _ _ _ _ _ _ of an illness.

II. Man or Machine?

In the past humans and machines were considered wholly separate entities. Today scientists study the automatic control system of both humans and machines in order to learn more about the science of control and communication: this is *cybernetics*. Other scientists specialize in the way humans operate in order to develop new and better machines: this is *bionics*. Sometimes a human and a machine work together very closely. For example, a man may be linked to a camera so that when he turns his head to the right, the camera—perhaps thousands of miles away—will also turn to the right to take a picture.

This combination of a human being and a machine is called a *cyborg*. If the *cyborg* is composed of a man wearing a metal suit that he can control, this metal structure is called an *exoskeleton*. If the human-shaped metal structure is not worn by a human but is controlled automatically, it is called a *robot*.

Match the terms in the first column with the definition or project in the second.

_ _ _ _ 1. bionics

_ _ _ _ 2. cybernetics

_ _ _ _ 3. cyborg

_ _ _ _ 4. exoskeleton

_ _ _ _ 5. robot

a. metal suit or framework shaped like a human being

b. machine that can clean house or pilot a satellite automatically

c. Someone studies the way a human leg bends and moves in order to make a more flexible machine.

d. A surgeon uses a mechanical arm over his own to perform a complicated operation.

e. Someone studies a computer and a human brain to learn more about memory retrieval.

III. Making a Man

Eugenics, scientific breeding in order to produce superior offspring, has long been practiced in the animal world. Now a few scientists are talking about *selective breeding* for people—choosing the healthiest and most intelligent men and women to produce superior children. Some have even more ambitious ideas. There is talk of *genetic manipulation* by which the genes that control heredity are added, changed, or removed for specific purposes. Supposedly it would then be possible to order a boy-child with a large bone structure, brown eyes, curly hair, and an I.Q. of 160! A process called *cloning* is even more farfetched. Through *cloning* it would be possible to copy one human being exactly. Imagine 10 of you—or 100! Here and there a scientist dreams of constructing a human being in a laboratory. These "possible" creatures are already being called *parahumans*.

Fill in each of the blanks below with one of the italicized terms from the paragraph above.

1. A procedure that would, in a sense, mimeograph human beings is _ _ _ _ _ _ _ _ _ _ _ _ _ _ _ _ _ _

_ .

2. A cattle rancher who hopes to develop a superior strain of cattle must know something about the science of _ .

3. Creatures that would look like human beings but that would be made, not born, are called _ .

4, 5. A government that wanted to weed out the weak in favor of the strong would probably try the process called _ , while a government that wanted to encourage several specific traits and eliminate several other specific traits would probably turn to _

_ _ _ _ _ _ _ _ _ _ _ _ _ _ .

IV. Other terms you should know:

____ 1. virus

____ 2. carcinogenic

____ 3. DNA

____ 4. chromosome

____ 5. mutation

____ 6. resuscitation

____ 7. conditioning

____ 8. heredity

____ 9. immunity

____ 10. life-support system

a. the passing on of characteristics from one generation to another

b. structure that penetrates living cells, often causing illness

c. bringing back to life of a "dead" or almost dead person

d. ability to resist infection

e. capable of causing cancer

f. training that tries to establish attitudes and values as well as behavior; often involves the reward system

g. macromolecule that contains the genetic code

h. certain machines (like the heart-lung machine) that are necessary to sustain life

i. In every human cell, there are 23 pairs of these; they carry DNA.

j. a change in the DNA, or genetic code, that results in a change of inherited characteristics

5
Puzzles for Posterity

Unlike most mysteries, these puzzles for posterity have no definite answers. The solutions rest in legal and moral decisions that have not yet been made—that *your* generation will have to make in the next few decades.

1. A man collapses of a heart attack. He stops breathing, and his heart stops beating. A skilled physician is in the next room. Before the doctor can begin trying to resuscitate the patient, the man's business partner strangles him. Is the partner guilty of murder?

   ---

2. A manufacturer needs a particular kind of person on the assembly line in his factory. He finds one person who is exactly right, and then orders—by cloning—50 identical people. A few weeks after they arrive, the manufacturer discovers that although each of the 51 people is docile, together they are quarrelsome. In one quarrel 10 of them kill one of the team. Who is responsible for the murder—the 10 "people," the manufacturer who ordered them, or the laboratory that actually developed them?

   ---

3. Bill and Dina Smith carefully planned their first son. They submitted specifications for his appearance, his I.Q., his talents, and his personality. Through genetic engineering the scientists were able to give them exactly the son they desired. Twenty years later Bill, Jr., was drinking too much, was taking drugs, and was generally unhappy. Could he sue his parents for providing an unsatisfactory recipe for *him*?

   ---

4. In outer space a spaceship from country A overtakes a spaceship from country B. Spaceship A steals all of the food from Spaceship B. In the absence of space law, is Spaceship A guilty of violating any law? What jury, if any, could decide? Would the problem be more or less difficult if one of the two spaceships had come from Mars instead of from Earth?

   ---

5. In a recent novel a patient who is violent is given an electrode implant by which his brain can be partly controlled by a computer. If something goes wrong with the computer and the patient then commits violence against another person, who is responsible—the patient, the surgeon who inserted the electrode, the analyst who set up the computer, or the computer that failed?

Nine. A Word for Everything

1
Animal Crackers

Animals provide us with food, clothing, and labor. (Animals, in this chapter, include birds, fish, and insects.) They are our pets and our assistants. Occasionally when we pamper them, they are our masters. It is not surprising then that they have played an important part in extending our language.

I. There are words that denote a particular kind of person. What kind of person is a

1. HOG? _____

2. JELLYFISH? _____

3. GOOSE? _____

4. SHARK? _____

5. CHAMELEON? _____

6. MULE? _____

7. FOX? _____

8. DONKEY? _____

9. SKUNK? _____

10. GADFLY? _____

Here's an interesting thought: MONKEY, BABOON, GORILLA, and APE are all used to describe certain kinds of human beings, and each word suggests something quite different. In one or two sentences, try to show exactly what is meant when a person uses each of these insults against another person.

11. MONKEY _____

12. BABOON _____

13. GORILLA _____

14. APE _____

II. Some cars are named after animals that have admirable qualities. List the characteristics of the following animals, after which cars have been named:

Mustang (Ford) _____

Charger (Dodge) _____

Barracuda (Chrysler) _____

Cougar (Mercury) --

Impala (Chevrolet) ---

III. Even our appearance and personalities are linked to animals. What does it mean if you

    1. have a horseface? --

    2. have the hide of a rhinoceros? ---

    3. wear a pigtail? --

    4. wear a ponytail? ---

    5. are eagle-eyed? --

    6. are lynx-eyed? ---

    7. have a cowlick? --

    8. are beetle-browed? ---

    9. are hawk-nosed? ---

  10. are lionhearted? ---

IV. Our actions are also described in terms of animal characteristics. What does it mean

    1. to wolf food? --

    2. to monkey with the machinery? ---

    3. to parrot a speech? --

    4. to eat crow? ---

    5. to ape an adult? ---

    6. to dog a suspect? --

    7. to weasel out of an agreement? ---

    8. to fox an opponent? --

    9. to rat on a comrade? ---

  10. to buffalo an enemy? ---

V. Whom are we imitating and what do we sound like if

    1. we cackle? ---

    2. we bark? ---

    3. we whinny? ---

    4. we bray? ---

    5. we growl? --

VI. And finally, there are names of animals that have totally different meanings. Can you match the animals with their "namesakes"?

---- 1. pony   *a.* flexible piece of metal, helpful in clearing drains

---- 2. eagle   *b.* small hidden microphone used for eavesdropping

---- 3. snake   *c.* top hat

---- 4. bug   *d.* word-for-word translation

---- 5. beaver   *e.* a golf score of two strokes less than par on a hole

2
Color Me Green!

Five letters—C O L O R—yet from them comes a whole dictionary of words! Consider:

She *colored* as the crowd rose to applaud her singing.
When he refused to help me, he was showing his true *colors*.
Don't yield if you are sure you are right; stick to your *colors!*
As the flagbearer led the way into battle, he raised the *colors* high.
You can *color* a story by emphasizing some points and omitting others.

I. Now you try some. If the colors of a particular fabric will not fade, it is said to be (1) color_ _ _ _ _ . If someone cannot tell red from green, he is (2) color_ _ _ _ _ _ . If a blouse has some red, some yellow, some green, and some purple in it, it is (3) color_ _ _ _ . If an essay is totally without excitement or interest, if it is drab and dull, it is (4) color_ _ _ _ _ . The military escort that surrounds the flag is called the (5) color _ _ _ _ _ _ . An artist who excels in the use of colors or to whom color is of prime importance is known as a (6) color_ _ _ . If you pass a test with a high grade, you say you have passed with (7) _ _ _ _ _ _ colors!

II. First, there's *green*. Can you find the "green" words or phrases that satisfy each definition?

> *Example:* a piece of paper money issued by the United States government
> *Answer:* greenback

---------------------------   1. an inexperienced person; a gullible person

---------------------------   2. jealous

---------------------------   3. a glass-enclosed structure where plants are grown all year round

---------------------------   4. permission to go ahead

---------------------------   5. ability to grow plants easily and well

III. Second, there's *red*.

---------------------------   1. in the act of committing a crime

---------------------------   2. a porter at a railroad station

---------------------------   3. vigorous; energetic

---------------------------   4. something that draws attention away from the main point

---------------------------   5. excessive paperwork that interferes with getting a job done

IV. Third, there's *blue*.

------------------------ 1. pertaining to a worker who works in a factory or who performs manual labor

------------------------ 2. an architectural drawing with white lines on a blue paper

------------------------ 3. a scholarly or pedantic woman

------------------------ 4. a sailor

------------------------ 5. to edit or revise written work

V. Fourth, there's *black*.

------------------------ 1. a small, leather-covered club on a strap

------------------------ 2. a scoundrel; a villainous person

------------------------ 3. the names of persons or groups that someone disapproves of

------------------------ 4. a material used to pave some roads

------------------------ 5. extinguishing of lights as a precaution against air raids

VI. Fifth, there's *white*.

------------------------ 1. a gift that may be expensive but that is difficult to use or maintain

------------------------ 2. pertaining to a worker, professional or clerical, who does not do manual labor

------------------------ 3. a small or diplomatic falsehood

------------------------ 4. a government report on any subject

------------------------ 5. a foamy crest of a wave

VII. Sixth, there are *assorted colors*.

------------------------ 1. newspaper reporting that emphasizes the sensational

------------------------ 2. a large dog with a narrow head and long legs; one that can run swiftly

------------------------ 3. a piece of noticeably ornate writing

------------------------ 4. thin squares of chocolate cake, often filled with nuts

------------------------ 5. a very long period of time

VIII. Can you think of colors that begin with "a," "b," and so on through the alphabet? You probably will not be able to find a "q" and a "z," but if you work hard enough, you can find all the others. (*Clue:* Don't forget gem, flower, and fruit colors.)

a _____   n _____

b _____   o _____

c _____   p _____

d _____   q _____

e _____   r _____

f _____   s _____

g _____   t _____

h _____   u _____

i _____   v _____

j _____   w _____

k _____   x _____

l _____   y _____

m _____   z _____

3
On Your Mettle!

On your *mettle* (prepared to do your best) about *metal*?
Then read on!

I. It was 1849 and the Gold Rush was on. Hopefuls came by the thousands from all over this
still raw country. *Prospectors* ranged the Rockies, sometimes in pairs, often alone. One
gold-seeker and his burro—that became the new pattern. Few of them knew anything
about *metallurgy*, but all were driven by the same fever that had excited the ancient
alchemists—GOLD!

Some were lucky. They found a rich *lode* and staked a claim—or they caught the glint
of *nuggets* lying in river beds or among the rocks. In town they carried these nuggets to
the *assayer's* office to be *appraised*.

Later—much later—the gold was *molded* into *ingots* or worked by *goldsmiths* into
rings and pendants. By then, though, the prospector and his burro were once again
wandering, hoping for a second meeting with Lady Luck.

By considering the context and by using the process of elimination, see if you can
match each of the following definitions with one of the italicized words above:

1. small lumps _____

2. in the Middle Ages especially, one who tried to change base metal into gold _____

_____

3. an artisan who fashions objects of gold _____

4. One explores an area looking for gold or some other precious substance. _____

_____

5. bars of metal shaped for easy handling and storage _____

6. the science of extracting metals from their ores, refining them, and preparing them

for use _____

7. one who analyzes for one or more valuable components _____

8. shaped, or formed _____

9. a vein of mineral ore; also, a rich supply _____

10. evaluated; judged _____

II. Seven metals—gold, silver, copper, tin, iron, lead, and mercury—were known about and
were used by people before 476 A.D. How effectively can *you* use these metals today?
In the blank or blanks below, fill in the word or words that satisfy each definition. Each
answer contains the name of one of the first seven metals.

_____ *a.* a woman who tries to get money or expensive
gifts from men

---------------------------- *b.* rigid and unyielding

---------------------------- *c.* utensils for use at the table

-------- --------- -------- *d.* composers and publishers of popular music, as a group

---------------------------- *e.* a hard white pottery

------------- ------------- *f.* a broken-down or cheap car

------------- - ------------ *g.* eloquent; able to persuade anyone to do anything

------------------- -------- *h.* a Northerner who aided the South during the Civil War

---------------------------- *i.* a planet and an automobile

---------------------------- *j.* dull and listless; a dark gray

III. What do we know about metals?

    We know that

        some are *extracted* (taken) from ores,

        some are *malleable* (capable of being shaped or formed),

        some are *brittle* (fragile; breakable; difficult to handle),

        and all, when polished, *reflect* (throw back) light.

    We also know

        that when two or more metals are combined, they form an *alloy*,

        that metals are melted and molded in *foundries*,

        and that the vessel that is strong enough to hold a melting metal is known as a *crucible*.

    Knowing the above, you should be able to apply that knowledge. Can you complete each of the following sentences by inserting in each blank one of the italicized words in the statements above?

1. Small children have minds so _____ that adults can easily shape their ideas and attitudes.

2. Copper and tin combine to form bronze, a(n) _____.

3. To alleviate (relieve) pain, the dentist _____ her impacted wisdom tooth.

4. Hair that is damaged becomes _____ and then is difficult to control.

5. The pond, like a sheet of silver, _____ the rays of the setting sun.

4
Jinks With Jewelry

In the Old Testament, Aaron (the brother of Moses) wore a breastplate decorated with 12 precious jewels. Each jewel was different, sparkling with its own light. Over the years people began to associate each jewel with a particular month of the year. So birthstones were born.

Since you have a birthstone and since your special jewel will bring you good luck (or so it is claimed), you certainly should know which one belongs to you. Here is a gem-wheel of birthstones. Note that in several cases there are two birthstones for one month.

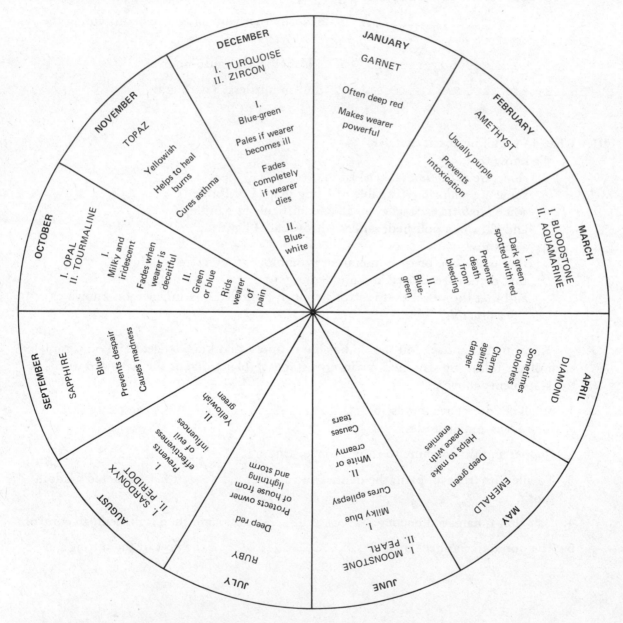

I. Which is your birthstone? _____

Wide World of Words

In the dictionary look up the definition, and copy it here so that you will know exactly what your birthstone is like.

II. Some gems are always one color, while others come in many colors. The following 10 are usually associated with a particular color. Can you match gem and color?

---- 1. ruby   *a.* dark green spotted with red jasper

---- 2. emerald   *b.* milky and iridescent

---- 3. amethyst   *c.* yellow

---- 4. topaz   *d.* deep red

---- 5. turquoise   *e.* black

---- 6. jet   *f.* purple

---- 7. bloodstone *g.* blue-green

---- 8. jade   *h.* blue

---- 9. sapphire   *i.* brilliant green

---- 10. opal   *j.* pale green

III. Checking the gem-wheel, try to deduce the correct answers to the following questions:

1. Of which gem did the ancient Romans make wine glasses? _ _ _ _ _ _ _ _ _ _ _ _ _ _ _ _ _ _

2. Which gem combined with "Isle" is used as an epithet for Ireland? _ _ _ _ _ _ _ _ _ _ _ _ _ _ _ _

3. Which gem gained its name from its resemblance to *seawater*? _ _ _ _ _ _ _ _ _ _ _ _ _ _ _ _ _ _ _

4. Which gem would you wear to monitor (keep check on) your health? _ _ _ _ _ _ _ _ _ _ _ _ _ _

5. Which gem is called the martyr's stone? _ _ _ _ _ _ _ _ _ _ _ _ _ _ _ _ _ _ _

IV. Pairs of gem-words. Try to place the following pairs correctly:

1. IMITATION—SYNTHETIC

    a. A(n) _ gem has the same chemical composition as a natural one but is made artificially.

    b. A(n) _ gem is made to resemble the natural one but is made of glass or paste.

2. CABOCHON CUT—FACET CUT
(*Cabochon* comes from a word meaning "cabbage," and *facet* from a word meaning "little face.")

    a. A _ _ _ _ _ _ _ _ _ _ _ _ _ _ _ _ _ _ _ cut yields a smooth, generally rounded surface.

b. A ──────────────── cut yields many tiny flat surfaces.

3. GEMOLOGIST—LAPIDARY

(A gemologist is a specialized student; a lapidary is a skilled craftsman.)

a. A ──────────────── is one who looks at stones critically, noting their quality, cut, color, authenticity, etc.

b. A ──────────────── is one who cuts, polishes, and engraves gems.

V. Five adjectives are used over and over again in describing gems. Can you match the adjectives in the first column with the expressions in the second?

──── 1. iridescent   *a.* radiant, bright; reflects light

──── 2. lustrous   *b.* Light can pass through it.

──── 3. opaque   *c.* many-colored, like a rainbow

──── 4. translucent   *d.* Light cannot pass through it.

──── 5. transparent   *e.* Light can pass through it, but distinct images do not.

    A *carat*, by the way, is a unit of weight for precious stones and gold. It is equal to 200 milligrams. Hence, the more carats, the heavier the gem or gold, and the more valuable.

VI. **To Test Your Deductive Powers**

1. What gem would be appropriate for a fireman with a respiratory problem? ──────── ────────────────

2. What is meant when one says that a technician monitors a TV picture? ─────────── ──

3. What exactly would be the difference between a sea described as jade green and one described as emerald green? ── ──

4. Why is the emerald especially appropriate for May? ──────────────────────── ──

5. Why would a superstitious person prefer a sardonyx? ─────────────────────── ──

6. A cat is often described as *topaz*. What color would it be? ────────────────────

7. Would the opal be a more likely candidate for a cabochon cut or a facet cut? ──────────────────────

8. Would a lapidarian inscription be found cut into stone or wood? ─────────

9. Considering the month of June specifically, can you guess one reason why some months have *two* birthstones rather than just one? _____

_____

_____

10. Which gem is exceedingly valuable even when it is colorless? _____

5
Flaunting Flowers

Everyone likes flowers, whether it's the elegant lily or the wild-growing dandelion. Flowers come in all sizes and shapes, in every conceivable color, in hothouses and in patches of soil never seen by a human being. One courtier will send his love an armful of roses; another will prefer the simplicity of a single rose.

I. A writer once said, "A rose is a rose is a rose . . .," but why is a rose called a rose? Both word and flower are so old that no one knows the origin; but for many flowers we do know how the names came into existence.

Below is a list of 10 common flowers and the origin of each name. Read it quickly; then see how many of the questions that follow the list you can answer.

a. aster — Greek, *aster* = star
b. dandelion — French, *dent de lion* = tooth of a lion
c. columbine — Latin, *columbinus* = dovelike
d. eglantine — Latin, *aculeus* = little needle
e. geranium — Greek, *geranion* = small crane
f. gladiolus — Latin, *gladius* = sword
g. heliotrope — Greek, *helio* = sun + *tropos* = turn
h. iris — Greek, *iris* = rainbow
i. nasturtium — Latin, *nasus* = nose + *tort* = twisted
j. tulip — Turkish, *tulbend* = turban

1. Which plant has a flower that resembles a crane's bill? _____

2. Which flower has varieties of almost every color? _____

3. Which flower is star-shaped? _____

4. Which flower has a pungent smell? _____

5. Which flower has sharply indented leaves? _____

6. Which flower always turns toward the sun? _____

7. Which flower, inverted, resembles a cluster of five doves? _____

8. Which flower looks a little like a turban? _____

9. Which flower is very prickly? _____

10. Which flower has sword-shaped leaves? _____

II. Some flowers have been named after people. By noting the spelling and probable pronunciation, try to name the flower that is a namesake of the following people:

1. Dr. Alexander Garden, Scottish naturalist   1. _____

2. Johann Gottfried Zinn, German botanist   2. _____

3. Caspar Wister, American anatomist   3. _____

4. Michel Bégon, governor of Santo Domingo   4. _____

5. Pierre Magnol, French botanist   5. _____

6. Georg Josef Kamel, Moravian Jesuit missionary   6. _____

7. Anders Dahl, Swedish botanist   7. _____

8. J. R. Poinsett, United States minister to Mexico   8. _____

9. Paion, physician of the Greek gods (mythological)   9. _____

10. Hyacinthus, Greek youth (mythological)   10. _____

III. Figures of speech using flowers are very common. Can you complete the following by inserting the name of a flower in each blank? (Use each flower only once.)

1. red as a _____

2. white as a _____

3. fresh as a _____

4. shrinking _____

5. _____ path

IV. Here are the names of five flowers:

| cornflower | marigold | snapdragon |
| cowslip | moonflower | |

Five intelligent guesses should enable you to use each of the above flowers to answer one of the questions below.

1. Which flower is found in pastures?   1. _____

2. Which flower resembles a legendary monster?   2. _____

3. Which flower blooms at night?   3. _____

4. Which flower grows on a farm?   4. _____

5. Which flower was named after the mother of Jesus?   5. _____

V. Your flower bed should now be a mass of blossoms. With the exercises you have already done in mind and with your general knowledge, can you provide the name of a plant for each of the letters below? (You should be able to complete at least 15 of the blanks.)

a_____   g_____

b_____   h_____

c_____   i_____

d_____   j_____

e_____   k_____

f_____   l_____

m _____ t _____

n _____ u _____

o _____ v _____

p _____ w _____

q _____ y _____

r _____ z _____

s _____

6
Vocations and Avocations

One's *vocation* is one's life's work. One's *avocation* is one's hobby—the way one fills leisure time. Most of us have one vocation and several avocations. Occasionally someone has an avocation that is more a habit than a hobby—the fellow who collects speeding tickets, for example, or the woman who attends parties to which she has not been invited.

Here are 35 descriptions of people with vocations, avocations, and near-avocations. Link each description with the doer. One who talks a lot without having the facts, for example, would be a *gossip*. See how many of the 35 you can get. If you have trouble, check the alphabetical list of answers at the end of the chapter for ideas.

1. one who serves as a member of a jury

1. _____

2. one who drinks too often and too much

2. _____

3. one who predicts future events

3. _____

4. one who announces a piece of news

4. _____

5. one who begins a lawsuit

5. _____

6. one who carries out court orders

6. _____

7. one who worries about little things

7. _____

8. one who keeps balls or ninepins circulating in the air

8. _____

9. one who commits bold or reckless criminal acts

9. _____

10. one who cuts and polishes gems

10. _____

11. one who rejects his party or cause

11. _____

12. one who specializes in the study of fish

12. _____

13. one who performs feats of balance and agility

13. _____

14. one to whom money is owed

14. _____

15. one who plays the violin

15. _____

16. one who jumps over obstacles in a race

16. _____

17. one who acts the fool to make people laugh

17. _____

18. one who navigates or helps to navigate a ship

18. _____

19. one who studies disorders of the nervous system

19. _____

20. one who goes fishing

20. _____

21. one who is well known and often referred to

21. _____

22. one who is skilled in horsemanship

22. _____

23. one who lives alone and prefers solitude

24. one who trims and sells women's hats

25. one who speaks so that his voice seems to come from someone else

26. one who works on very high structures

27. one who administers ether, chloroform, cocaine, etc., to a patient to make him insensitive to pain

28. one who negotiates stock purchases and sales

29. one who delivers messages for a government

30. one who receives and sells stolen goods

31. one who goes to a party without being invited

32. one who uses X rays to form a medical diagnosis

33. one authorized by law to attest the authenticity of a signature

34. one who has no regular home or income

35. one who samples food or drink for quality

23. _____

24. _____

25. _____

26. _____

27. _____

28. _____

29. _____

30. _____

31. _____

32. _____

33. _____

34. _____

35. _____

Glossary of Terms

acrobat	hurdler	notary public
anesthetist	ichthyologist	plaintiff
angler	jester	radiologist
broker	juggler	renegade
celebrity	juror	soothsayer
courier	lapidary	steeplejack
creditor	mariner	taster
desperado	marshal	tippler
equestrian	milliner	vagrant
fence	neurologist	ventriloquist
fiddler		
fussbudget		
gate-crasher		
herald		
hermit		

7

Worked-over Words

Some words are overworked; others can be worked over. You can work over words by combining them with other words or by adding prefixes or suffixes to make new words. Using the definitions provided as a guide, try "working over" the words listed below.

I. Line

1. a ball batted sharply and accurately (2 words)
2. a plan, or sketch
3. official policy (2 words)
4. list of ancestors

1. line _ _ _ _ _ _
2. _ _ _ _line
3. _ _ _ _ _ _ _ line
4. line_ _ _ _

II. Grand

1. the female parent of one's parent
2. a long trip around Europe (2 words)
3. a roofed area for spectators
4. elaborate drama set to music (2 words)
5. theft of valuable property (2 words)

1. grand_ _ _ _ _ _ _ _
2. grand _ _ _ _ _ _
3. grand_ _ _ _ _ _ _
4. grand _ _ _ _ _ _ _
5. grand _ _ _ _ _ _ _ _ _

III. Out

1. sudden eruption
2. criminal excluded from society
3. protest, or loud objection
4. disgraceful; appalling
5. to leave behind; to surpass

1. out_ _ _ _ _ _ _
2. out_ _ _ _
3. out_ _ _ _
4. out_ _ _ _ _ _ _ _ _
5. out_ _ _ _ _ _

IV. Stock

1. animals raised on a farm
2. one who owns shares in a company
3. a permanent group of actors (2 words)
4. fenced-in area used for protection
5. material stored for future use

1. _ _ _ _ _stock
2. stock_ _ _ _ _ _ _ _
3. stock _ _ _ _ _ _ _ _ _ _
4. stock_ _ _ _
5. stock_ _ _ _ _

V. Time

1. a watch or clock
2. hour to retire
3. eternal; endless
4. trite; overused
5. recess; short break

1. time_ _ _ _ _ _
2. _ _ _ _time
3. time_ _ _ _ _
4. time_ _ _ _ _
5. time-_ _ _ _

VI. Sign

1. gesture or sound meant to communicate
2. name of a person, written by self
3. secret sign or password
4. meaningful; important
5. seal used on a document

1. sign_ _ _
2. sign_ _ _ _ _ _
3. _ _ _ _ _ _ _ _sign
4. sign_ _ _ _ _ _ _ _
5. sign_ _ _

VII. Land

1. first sight of land from a ship or plane
2. person who rents rooms or buildings to others
3. a view or painting of natural scenery
4. the falling down of a large mass of rock or earth
5. a boundary line, historical building, or major event in history

1. land_ _ _ _ _ _
2. land_ _ _ _ _
3. land_ _ _ _ _ _
4. land_ _ _ _ _ _
5. land_ _ _ _ _

VIII. To Test Your Deductive Powers

Here are five of the words encountered in this chapter:

grand opera	landmark	livestock
grand tour	landslide	

Below are five sentences. Each can be completed sarcastically by inserting the appropriate word in the blank. (*Sarcasm*, remember, is mocking or contemptuous language.) In each case insert the correct word; then explain why it is used sarcastically.

1. The town was so small the visitor completed a _ _ _ _ _ _ _ _ _ _ _ _ _ _ _ _ _ _ of it in

   three minutes. _

   _

   _

2. Because the half dozen servants were too dependent on him, the butler referred to

   them contemptuously as his _ _ _ _ _ _ _ _ _ _ _ _ _ _ _ _ _ . _ _ _ _ _ _ _ _ _ _ _ _ _ _ _

_____

_____

3. Having won a majority of three out of a million votes cast, the politician calmly

   claimed a _____ victory. _____

   _____

   _____

4. The sole _____ of Tardy Tim's career at Milton High will be

   remembered forever—the day he got to school on time! _____

   _____

   _____

5. With the stereo blazing in the background, our next-door neighbors' daily quarrels

   sounded like a _____ . _____

   _____

   _____

8
Body-Building

Among the first words a child learns are the words that name parts of his body: eye, ear, foot, hand. Because these words are so well known, they have been used in many different ways.

Here is a list of the most often-used words that name body parts:

arm	eye	heart	mouth
brow	face	heel	neck
chin	finger	knee	nose
ear	foot	leg	thumb
elbow	hand	lip	toe

All of the following exercises use the 20 words listed above.

I. Complete each of the following phrases by inserting one of the 20 words. Do not use any word more than once.

1. _____ of a chair

2. _____ of a clock

3. _____ of corn

4. _____ of a potato

5. _____ of a shoe

6. _____ of a bed

7. _____ of the matter

8. _____ of a hill

9. _____ of a river

10. _____ of land

II. Each of the following phrases defines a vivid expression naming one of the body parts. Again, do not use any word more than once.

1. to walk or run   = to _____ it

2. to snoop; to meddle = to _____ into

3. to rant; to declaim = to _____

4. to talk a lot; to chatter = to _____

5. to follow closely   = to _____

III. The following popular expressions can be completed by inserting the names of the appropriate body parts. Each word is to be used only once.

1. to keep an _____ to the ground (to watch current trends closely)

2. to follow one's _____ (to go straight ahead)

3. to _ _ _ _ _ _ _ _ _ _ _ up to (to recognize a problem; to confront)

4. with open _ _ _ _ _ _ _ _ _ _ (cordially; with friendliness)

5. to take to one's _ _ _ _ _ _ _ _ _ _ (to run away)

IV. Complete each word in the first column after reading the definitions in the second column.

1. hand_ _ _ _ _ _ _ _   manacles to secure a prisoner

2. foot_ _ _ _ _   low part of a mountain

3. leg_ _ _ _ _ _   leather or canvas covering from knee to foot

4. ear_ _ _ _ _ _   a piece of jewelry for the ear

5. eye_ _ _ _ _ _ _ _ _   someone who has seen a crime committed

6. neck_ _ _ _ _ _ _ _ _ _   kind of scarf worn around the neck

7. toe_ _ _ _ _ _   small ledge useful when climbing

8. nose _ _ _ _ _ _   sudden downward plunge (2 words)

9. hand_ _ _ _ _ _ _ _   skilled trade; articles made by one skilled in working with his hands

10. knee_ _ _ _ _ _   opening under a desk

11. elbow _ _ _ _ _ _ _ _   hard physical effort (2 words)

12. finger_ _ _ _ _ _ _   impression of fingertip made with ink

13. foot_ _ _ _ _ _ _   free to do as one likes

14. thumb_ _ _ _ _   small, short nail often used on bulletin boards

15. heart_ _ _ _ _ _   central and vital part of a country

Ten. You're Twisting My Words

1

Be a Name-Dropper

Riddle: What is owned by you but used mostly by others?
Answer: Your name.

Your name, whether you like it or dislike it, is an important part of you, almost as distinctive a characteristic as your hair or your eyes. That makes the whole process of naming serious business, but—human nature being what it is—it also provides some good source material for wordplay.

I. Many first names (the full names or shortened forms) have a special meaning of their own when they are not capitalized. Olive, for example, is a small fruit used as a relish, but it is also a girl's name. See if you can match the names in the first column with the definitions in the second column.

____	1.	Bill	a.	night before a holiday
____	2.	Victor	b.	to take someone to law for compensation
____	3.	Ruth	c.	British nobleman
____	4.	Sue	d.	place where rabbits breed
____	5.	Penny	e.	a record of goods sold, showing the cost
____	6.	Earl	f.	mercy; compassion
____	7.	Violet	g.	one who wins a contest
____	8.	Gene	h.	one-cent piece
____	9.	Eve	i.	unit in the body that controls heredity
____	10.	Warren	j.	small purplish blue flower

II. Sometimes first names do not have a second meaning until they are scrambled. GERALD, for example, means only GERALD; but change the letter order, and it suddenly means GLARED. See if you can identify the names in the following sentences by unscrambling the italicized clues.

1. Since this girl was interested in national defense, she joined the *army* after she graduated from high school. Her name is _____ .

2. This boy likes to *wander*. He may settle down later and become the *warden* of a prison. His name is _____ .

3. This girl likes to *take* trips to India to buy furniture made of *teak*. Her name is _____ _____ .

4. This boy loves *rice*—curried, creamed, or plain. His name is _____ .

5. Although this girl owns several *horses*, she favors her *roan* mare. Her name is _____ .

6. When this boy first took up carpentry, he was shocked to discover one day that he had *nailed* his shoe to the floor. His name is _____ .

7. This girl, who has studied scientific agriculture, analyzes *soil* and lives in a *silo*. Her name is _____ .

8. A would-be architect, this boy hopes to *raze* ugly buildings and raise new ones. His name is _____ .

9. This girl, who likes to *hoard* money, plans to become a banker. Her name is _____ .

10. Since her home is at the shore, it is natural that this girl likes to *sail* boats. Her name is _____ .

III. Names of countries often combine with other words to create interesting names of things. Everyone knows *Canadian* bacon and *Irish* stew, for example. Complete each of the following phrases by inserting the correct foreign city, country, etc. The clues in parentheses should help you.

1. _____ heels (medium height and thickness)
2. _____ treat (Everyone pays his own way.)
3. _____ cheese (with holes)
4. _____ shorts (almost to the knee)
5. _____ toast (dipped in egg and milk)
6. _____ dressing (mayonnaise with chili sauce, etc.)
7. _____ blinds (slatted window screens)
8. _____ checkers (played with marbles)
9. _____ pastry (sweet and buttery)
10. _____ sprouts (small cabbages)

IV. American place-names can be used in the same way. How many of these can you complete?

1. _____ Red (domestic fowl with reddish brown feathers)
2. _____ cream pie (cake with custard filling)
3. _____ clam chowder (made with tomatoes and thyme)

4. _____ reel (a country dance)

5. _____ cheer (shows contempt)

6. _____ lawyer (especially shrewd and subtle)

7. _____ beds (conducive to dreams)

8. _____ blues (jazz, Missouri style)

9. _____ cottage (lovely to stay there in the summer)

10. _____ oriole (bright orange, black, and white, the colors of

Lord _____)

2
Forward-Reverse

Words are symbols—they mean what we want them to mean. That is why some words can mean one thing when you read from left to right, and something quite different when you read from right to left.

I. In the exercise below, (1) refers to the left-to-right reading, and (2) refers to the right-to-left reading. How many of these three-letter words can *you* identify?

> *Example:* What word means (1) a piece, and (2) a snare?
> *Answer:* part—trap

1. _____ _____ What word means (1) a short sleep, and (2) a shallow cooking vessel?

2. _____ _____ What word means (1) a conflict, and (2) not cooked?

3. _____ _____ What word means (1) a deep hole, and (2) a gratuity?

4. _____ _____ What word means (1) a water barrier, and (2) insane?

5. _____ _____ What word means (1) an historical age, and (2) exist?

6. _____ _____ What word means (1) an up-and-down movement of the head, and (2) to put on?

7. _____ _____ What word means (1) a rodent, and (2) a black sticky substance?

8. _____ _____ What word means (1) to fasten, and (2) to bite just a little?

9. _____ _____ What word means (1) to scratch or damage, and (2) a male sheep?

10. _____ _____ What word means (1) 2,000 pounds, and (2) a negative adverb?

II. This time the correct answers will be four-letter words. How many of these can you identify?

1. _____ _____ What word means (1) a game played on the green, and (2) to beat, or whip?

2. _____ _____ What word means (1) a wild canine, and (2) a stream, or outpouring?

3. _____ _____ What word means (1) dull, not bright, and (2) a poet?

4. _____ _____ What word means (1) a small, annoying insect, and (2) a sharp, distinctive flavor?

5. _____ _____ What word means (1) the feet of an animal, and (2) to trade, or exchange?

6. _____ _____ What word means (1) to revise or correct, and (2) a regular change in water level?

7. _____ _____ What word means (1) a terrible fate, and (2) the state of one's feelings?

8. _____ _____   What word means (1) a track or horizontal bar, and (2) one who does not tell the truth?

9. _____ _____   What word means (1) to boast, and (2) clothing?

10. _____ _____   What word means (1) an animal with antlers, and (2) a hollow stalk?

III. This time the correct answers are words with five, six, seven, or eight letters. These are considerably more difficult. How many of these can you identify?

1. _____ _____   What word means (1) fractions or sections, and (2) a long, narrow piece of leather?

2. _____ _____   What word means (1) clever, bright, shrewd, and (2) British streetcars?

3. _____ _____   What word means (1) joins closely or unites securely, and (2) a bad odor?

4. _____ _____   What word means (1) to send money, and (2) something or someone that measures time?

5. _____ _____   What word means (1) a coarse cloth or overall, and (2) excavated from the earth?

6. _____ _____   What word means (1) a garment for a baby, and (2) made a return payment?

7. _____ _____   What word means (1) emphasized, or accented, and (2) after-dinner sweets?

8. _____ _____   What word means (1) to send or to rescue, and (2) abused, or denounced?

9. _____ _____   What word means (1) something received for meritorious behavior, and (2) a sliding compartment in furniture?

10. _____ _____   What word means (1) to take great delight, and (2) a metal bar used to lift weights?

3
Cracking the Code

Consider this:

B sounds like *be* sounds like *bee* sounds like *Bea*. Letters have sounds that are sometimes identical to word sounds. Because this is true, a simple (though limited) code can be used, having letters replace words. "A B is bothering B," translated, means that "a bee is bothering Bea"! A double letter can form a plural (e.g., BB = bees) or a totally new word (e.g., TT = tease).

Ready to try it? After each coded statement, write out the correct translation.

1. Consumed by NV, B joined the Q to buy some T.

   ----

2. "I, I, sir," said the sailor, as the ship put out to C.

   ----

3. Some CD characters R in the MT building.

   ----

4. J used all of his NRG to write an SA about BB.

   ----

5. "Making a TP is EZ," said Jim.

   ----

6. The BD II of the J made him seem YY.

Now add number codes for increased mystification. *2*, for example, is *to*, or *too*, or *two*.

7. "Do not work 2 XS," said the YY man. "B at EE."

   ----

8. Trying 2 lose weight, she 8 only a P for dinner.

   ----

9. If U TT a B, B ready 2 run.

   ----

10. In the MT L of the IC barn, a U vainly searched 4 her lamb.

    ----

11. The young actress entered on Q, recited her lines with EE, and 1 applause.

    ----

12. "O Y did U go 2 C?" cried the lonely mother.

    ----

13. Because he 8 sweets 2 XS, he suffered tooth DK.

For an added fillip (touch of excitement; stimulus), consider the code value of the tones of the musical scale: do, re, mi, fa, sol, la, ti, do. Note how they *sound*, not how they look. For example, *do = doe* or *dough*.

14. The do 4 the bread did not rise.

----

15. The re of the sun hit my I, and I could not C fa.

----

16. If U XL in spelling, help mi, 4 I do not find it EZ.

As a final twist, code *syllables* as well as words. For example, *2day = today*.

17. The do and the U 8 2gether.

----

18. The blue JJ EZ flights R the NV of the bumbleBB.

----

19. Y did U buy a toy 2 big 4 the baB?

----

20. As I headed 4 the T 2 C if the EZ course was MT, I heard 1 member of a 4some shout "4!"

Now U try writing in code. Make up a complicated message and code it. Later Xchange your coded message with a friend's and C if U can Dcode each other's.

4
Which Is the Kate That . . . ?

Twenty-six letters (the alphabet) can be combined to form millions of words. Even so, a few combinations occur over and over, for they are especially versatile.

I. Consider *ace*, for example. There's f*ace*—or l*ace*—or disgr*ace*. Find the *-ace* words for the following definitions:

1. a location; a spot

1. _ _ _ _ _ _ _ _ _ _ _ _ _ _ _

2. a competition

2. _ _ _ _ _ _ _ _ _ _ _ _ _ _ _

3. a hint; something left

3. _ _ _ _ _ _ _ _ _ _ _ _ _ _ _

4. a facial distortion

4. _ _ _ _ _ _ _ _ _ _ _ _ _ _ _

5. the people in an area; people as a whole

5. _ _ _ _ _ _ _ _ _ _ _ _ _ _ _

II. It all becomes more complicated when the definitions appear in rhyme. Here are a few *and* words that properly rearranged will help to make sense of each line of verse.

ampersand	contraband	strand
bland	hand	understand
command	reprimand	

Which is the *and* that chides and scolds

1. _ _ _ _ _ _ _ _ _ _ _ _ _ _ _ _ _ _ _

The *and* that has back and palm,

2. _ _ _ _ _ _ _ _ _ _ _ _ _ _ _ _ _ _ _

The *and* that is loved by smugglers bold,

3. _ _ _ _ _ _ _ _ _ _ _ _ _ _ _ _ _ _ _

The *and* that is gentle and calm?

4. _ _ _ _ _ _ _ _ _ _ _ _ _ _ _ _ _ _ _

Which is the *and* that means just "and,"

5. _ _ _ _ _ _ _ _ _ _ _ _ _ _ _ _ _ _ _

The *and* that borders the sea,

6. _ _ _ _ _ _ _ _ _ _ _ _ _ _ _ _ _ _ _

The *and* that means "to comprehend,"

7. _ _ _ _ _ _ _ _ _ _ _ _ _ _ _ _ _ _ _

The *and* for the king's decree?

8. _ _ _ _ _ _ _ _ _ _ _ _ _ _ _ _ _ _ _

III. Try it with names—with Ed, for example. Here's one.

bed	red	sled
coed	shed	wed
fled	shred	

Which is the *Ed* that ran from his foe,

1. _ _ _ _ _ _ _ _ _ _

The *Ed* that's a cute college girl,

2. _ _ _ _ _ _ _ _ _ _

The *Ed* that's a tatter of cloth, rather small,

3. _ _ _ _ _ _ _ _ _ _

The *Ed* that got hitched in a whirl?

4. _ _ _ _ _ _ _ _ _ _

Which is the *Ed* that runs over snow,   5. _ _ _ _ _ _ _ _ _ _

The *Ed* that's the color of sin,   6. _ _ _ _ _ _ _ _ _ _

The *Ed* that's a building, small and detached,   7. _ _ _ _ _ _ _ _ _ _

The *Ed* that it's good to fall in!   8. _ _ _ _ _ _ _ _ _ _

IV. *Ray* is fairly versatile. Try this.

betray	gray	stray
disarray	portray	tray
fray	spray	

Which is the *Ray* that's not dark or bright,   1. _ _ _ _ _ _ _ _ _ _ _ _ _ _ _

The *Ray* that waters the prow,   2. _ _ _ _ _ _ _ _ _ _ _ _ _ _ _

The *Ray* that contains both the tea and the cake,   3. _ _ _ _ _ _ _ _ _ _ _ _ _ _ _

The *Ray* that's a maverick cow?   4. _ _ _ _ _ _ _ _ _ _ _ _ _ _ _

Which is the *Ray* that gives aid to the foe,   5. _ _ _ _ _ _ _ _ _ _ _ _ _ _ _

The *Ray* that unravels the cloth,   6. _ _ _ _ _ _ _ _ _ _ _ _ _ _ _

The *Ray* that depicts a man's actions or face,   7. _ _ _ _ _ _ _ _ _ _ _ _ _ _ _

The *Ray* that disorder has wrought?   8. _ _ _ _ _ _ _ _ _ _ _ _ _ _ _

V. But the really versatile gal is Kate—though spelled with a "c." Here's a real puzzler for you!

abdicate	fabricate	prevaricate
communicate	indicate	reciprocate
complicate	intoxicate	suffocate
domesticate	lubricate	vacate
eradicate	placate	vindicate
extricate		

Which is the *Kate* that absolves you of guilt,   1. _ _ _ _ _ _ _ _ _ _ _ _ _ _ _ _ _

The *Kate* that befuddles your wit,   2. _ _ _ _ _ _ _ _ _ _ _ _ _ _ _ _ _

The *Kate* that tells fibs with a persuasive lilt,   3. _ _ _ _ _ _ _ _ _ _ _ _ _ _ _ _ _

The *Kate* that points out that that's *it*?   4. _ _ _ _ _ _ _ _ _ _ _ _ _ _ _ _ _

Which is the *Kate* that erases with glee,   5. _ _ _ _ _ _ _ _ _ _ _ _ _ _ _ _ _

The *Kate* that converses and chats,   6. _ _ _ _ _ _ _ _ _ _ _ _ _ _ _ _ _

The *Kate* that teaches to trade mutually,   7. _ _ _ _ _ _ _ _ _ _ _ _ _ _ _ _ _

The *Kate* that turns lions to cats?   8. _ _ _ _ _ _ _ _ _ _ _ _ _ _ _ _ _

Which is the *Kate* that gives up the throne,   9. -------------------------

The *Kate* that makes simple things *not*,   10. -------------------------

The *Kate* that can quiet a dog with a bone,   11. -------------------------

The *Kate* that abandons a spot?   12. -------------------------

Which is the *Kate* that will oil the car's gears,   13. -------------------------

The *Kate* that can fables create,   14. -------------------------

The *Kate* that will free you from dangers and fears,   15. -------------------------

The *Kate* that will smother poor Kate?   16. -------------------------

5 Words Within Words

It is possible to dissect a word and find in it one or more smaller words—sort of instant progeny! (*Progeny*, as you may know, means "children" or "offspring.") In *panel*, for example, you can find a *pan*, in *manual* a *man*.

I. See if you can help to furnish a house from the following words:

1. In *obedience*, you can find a _____ .

2. In *computable*, you can find a _____ .

3. In *druggist*, you can find a _____ .

4. In *clamped*, you can find a _____ ,

5. and in *stubble*, you can find a _____ .

Or construct a human being from these:

6. In *sweetheart*, you can find a _____ .

7. In *deface*, you can find a _____ .

8. In *chinchilla*, you can find a _____ .

9. In *allegiance*, you can find a _____ ,

10. and in *farmer*, you can find a(n) _____ .

Or find something to eat in these:

11. In *corollary*, you can find a _____ .

12. In *brother*, you can find some _____ .

13. In *shamrock*, you can find some _____ .

14. In *screaming*, you can find a little _____ ,

15. and in *instead*, you can find some _____ .

II. Now you're ready for something a good deal more challenging. Suppose you were asked if you could find an *insect* and a *bird* in a pair of britches. With a little detective work, you should be able to come up with the answer: an *ant* and a *loon* in *pantaloons*!

Below are 15 words. Each of them will help you in making "words from words." (Note: The words may overlap as do *era* and *rat* in *operation*.)

appointment	kidnapping	penitentiary
assignation	lieutenant	plumber
bayonet	manslaughter	sergeant
factory	palace	spear
general	paperhanger	treason

1. Find a body of water and a device for catching fish in a weapon.

   _____ and _____ in _____

2. Find a fruit and a vegetable in a weapon.

   _____ and _____ in _____

3. Find a fruit and some wood in a workingman who works indoors.

   _____ and _____ in _____

4. Find a simian and an emotion in a workingman who works indoors.

   _____ and _____ in _____

5. Find a beast of burden and an omen in a planned meeting.

   _____ and _____ in _____

6. Find a sharp end and a salve in a planned meeting.

   _____ and _____ in _____

7. Find a fabric and an insect in a military man.

   _____ and _____ in _____

8. Find a renter and a falsehood in a military man.

   _____ and _____ in _____

9. Find a carrier of heredity and an historical age in a military man.

   _____ and _____ in _____

10. Find a writing instrument and camping equipment in a large building.

    _____ and _____ in _____

11. Find a division of a play and a rocky cliff in a large building.

    _____ and _____ in _____

12. Find a close friend and a playing card in a large building.

    _____ and _____ in _____

13. Find a young goat and a brief sleep in a crime.

    _____ and _____ in _____

14. Find an adult male and a mirthful expression in a crime.

    _____ and _____ in _____

15. Find the power to think and a male offspring in a crime.

    _____ and _____ in _____

6
Bittersweet

People are contrary. We like to think in opposites. Try this word association test:

What word do you think of when you hear the word "open?"
Probably you chose the antonym of *open*, that is, *shut*.
Try another:
What word do you think of when you hear the word "day?"
Again you probably chose the antonym *night*.
Why do we do this? No one knows. It's a quirk in our human nature. Opposites attract.

I. Some opposites, or *antonyms*, are fascinating in their appearance. What is ironical about the appearance of these two pairs of antonyms?

1.
```
        L
        I              S
        T       H      T
    B   T       O      A
    I   L       R      L
    G   E       T      L
```

----

2. Some are intriguing in their sound. Consider the lulling sound of *asleep* and the quick sharp sound of *awake*. Comment on the appropriateness of the *sounds* of the following pairs of antonyms:

a. *sick* and *well*: --

----

b. *beginning* and *end*: --------------------------------------

----

----

c. *alive* and *dead*: ---

----

d. *bright* and *dark*: --

----

e. *open* and *shut*: --

II. Antonyms are made in a number of ways. One common way is simply to add a prefix. *Un* + *common*, for example, gives us *uncommon*; *in* + *decent* gives us *indecent*. There are several prefixes that create antonyms: *un, in, il, ir, non,* and *dis* are the most common.

Below are 20 words. Next to each one write the antonym that can be formed by adding the proper prefix. Then write a brief definition of each antonym. (Some you may know; some you may have to look up in the dictionary.)

	Antonym	Definition of Antonym
1. fortunate		
2. legal		
3. valid		
4. stop		
5. trust		
6. responsible		
7. orthodox		
8. relevant		
9. fiction		
10. legible		
11. entangle		
12. significant		
13. literate		
14. resolute		
15. wary		
16. combatant		
17. compatible		
18. conditional		
19. partisan		
20. reconcilable		

III. In some pairs of antonyms, *both* words have prefixes—antonymous prefixes. A junior or senior is an *upper*classman, while a freshman or sophomore is a *lower*classman. In addition to *upper* and *lower*, some antonymous prefixes are *up* and *down*, *high* and *low*, *over* and *under*. Add antonymous prefixes to each of the following words. After each pair of antonyms thus formed, describe briefly the difference between the two words.

1. _____ stream   _____ stream

_____

_____

2. ---------- grade   ---------- grade

----

3. ---------- pass   ---------- pass

----

4. ---------- swing   ---------- swing

----

5. ---------- boy   ---------- boy

IV. Still other antonymous phrases are formed by adding opposing words.

1. One reporter decides to *play up* a story; another plans to *play down* the same story. How does each handle the story?

----

2. One sister *takes on* a new job; the other sister *takes off* a 20% discount. What does each do?

----

3. Your father has *run up* a bill; your clock has *run down*. What has each done?

But strange things can happen when you handle words. Sometimes antonymous helpers change the words entirely, leaving separate phrases that are entirely unrelated.

4. You *dress up* for dinner, but *dress down* a friend who has made a mistake. What did you do in each case?

----

5. One salesman *oversells*; the other salesman *undersells*. What has each done?

----

6. You *overtake* your opponent in a competition, but you *undertake* a new project. What did you do in each case?

V. Each of the following italicized words or pairs of words is unusual, sometimes illogical. In each case try to spot the oddity, and describe it briefly.

1. Naturally, the chicken weighed less after it was *dressed*.

----

2. After he *unloosed* his jacket, he *loosed* his tie.

----

3. The waltz, a *graceful* dance, was once regarded as *disgraceful*.

----

4. Gasoline is *flammable*; kerosene is *inflammable*.

----

5. He was at *ease* although he had been stricken by a tropical *disease*.

----

6. Purple was the *color* of the *discoloration*.

----

7. Louisa *assumed* an *unassuming* pose.

----

8. The woman, *unnerved* by the explosion, fought to gain control of her *nerves*.

7

Patterns to Ponder

Being a detective with words is no easy task. It demands a recognition of patterns and a sensitivity to the breaking of those patterns. It demands a versatile and alert *awareness*.

I. In this exercise there are 10 groups of words. Each group has its own pattern, but one word in each group violates the pattern. There are 5 kinds of patterns in these 10 groups:

   a. double letters, e.g., ru*dd*er, ba*tt*le
   b. two-letter sequences, e.g., *pl*ease, *pl*ay
   c. two-letter sequences split, e.g., f*ir*e, p*in*e
   d. three-letter sequences, e.g., por*tra*y, *tra*mp
   e. four-letter sequences, e.g., *gram*mar, dia*gram*

   In each group below, identify the pattern and isolate the word that does not fit the pattern.

   1. little, raccoon, coordinate, later, crossword

      ----

   2. milligram, demented, lemon, mundane, humanity

      ----

   3. toaster, startle, restless, destination, tearfulness

      ----

   4. compare, tamper, caret, carefulness, stared

      ----

   5. babble, guess, flower, reentry, dipper

      ----

   6. boldly, paddle, womanly, childlike, treadle

      ----

   7. acorn, according, cornucopia, unicorn, scornful

      ----

   8. decal, lecture, nickle, calculation, scold

      ----

   9. prominent, prevalent, coming, ominous, dominion

      ----

   10. retail, taint, tatters, certainly, tailored

II. This exercise is more sophisticated. Each of the four groups includes four titles and authors. In each group there is a pattern. Consider this example:

> *The Grapes of Wrath* by Steinbeck
> *Huckleberry Finn* by Twain
> *Picnic* by Inge
> *The Cherry Orchard* by Chekhov

In this group the first, second, and fourth titles include the name of a fruit. The third does not.

Now you try it. In each of the following four groups identify the pattern and isolate the "maverick":

1. *a.* *The Glass Menagerie* by Williams
   b. *The Zoo Story* by Albee
   c. *Animal Farm* by Orwell
   d. *The Way of All Flesh* by Butler

   ----

2. *a.* *The Tempest* by Shakespeare
   b. *The Skin of Our Teeth* by Wilder
   c. *Heart of Darkness* by Conrad
   d. *The Eye of the Hurricane* by Buckley

   ----

3. *a.* *The Forsythe Saga* by Galsworthy
   b. *A Tale of Two Cities* by Dickens
   c. "The Cask of Amontillado" by Poe
   d. "The Legend of Sleepy Hollow" by Irving

   ----

4. *a.* "The Purloined Letter" by Poe
   b. "Ali Baba and the Forty Thieves"
   c. *The Embezzler* by Auchincloss
   d. *The War of the Worlds* by Wells

III. This third exercise is the most sophisticated of all. Here each group of words has a pattern, but you are given no hint at all as to what that pattern is. It may be in the meanings of the words, in their structure, in their sound, in the letter order. Can you identify each pattern and the one word that doesn't conform to it?

1. gerrymander, ballot, politician, terrible, keepsake

   ----

2. return, reader, revile, restrain, recall

   ----

3. cordon, cigar, khaki, kitten, color

   ----

4. bolero, cardigan, dirndl, cravat, crepe

   ----

5. marriage, drama, sleeve, tunic, bookcase

   ----

6. comfort, decoy, solace, menace, intact

   ----

7. gigantic, enormous, minute, massive, colossal

   ----

8. nimble, stiff, agile, brisk, sprightly

   ----

9. locate, catastrophe, dictate, caterer, scatter

   ----

10. partisan, adversary, antagonist, opponent, enemy

8
Happiness Is . . . a Warm Puppy

Dictionaries give good, solid, meaningful definitions, but often they do not capture the *whole* meaning of a word. *Happiness*, according to most dictionaries, is the state of well-being and contentment, of being pleased. It's accurate, but for a deeper human meaning, for a richer understanding, we turn to something more informal: "Happiness is a warm puppy." This simple comparison does what the accurate definition could not do: it surrounds the word with associations and memories that clarify and enlarge the meaning.

I. The definitions below have been thought out carefully by some very human human beings. Try to match each of the words listed with one of the definitions. You will find that you must think as a *human* rather than as a *student*. In other words, you must bring sensitivity to scholarship.

acquaintance	history	puritan
antique	hope	rudeness
architecture	love	saints
caterpillar	man	silence
city life	modesty	speculator
cold war	news	speech
committee	(the) obvious	thrift
detour	prayer	total eclipse
experience	professions	vulgarity
(a) father	psychoanalysis	weed

1. _____: an upholstered worm (Anonymous)

2. _____: nations flexing their missiles (D. O. Flynn)

3. _____: the only animal that blushes—or needs to (Mark Twain)

4. _____: an object that has made a round trip to the attic (*Denver Post*)

5. _____: common sense applied to spending (Theodore Roosevelt)

6. _____: the unwilling, selected from the unsuitable, to do the unnecessary (Anonymous)

7. _____: frozen music (Goethe)

8. _____: a plant whose virtues have not yet been discovered (Ralph Waldo Emerson)

9. _____: a wish turned heavenward (Phillips Brooks)

10. _____: millions of people being lonesome together (Henry D. Thoreau)

11. _____: the great dust heap (Augustine Birrell)

12. _____: the garlic in the salad of taste (Cyril Connolly)

13. _____: a man who observes the future and acts before it occurs (Bernard Baruch)

14. _____: the affirmative of affirmatives (Ralph Waldo Emerson)

15. _____: the name we give our mistakes (Oscar Wilde)

16. _____: sinners who keep on trying (Robert Louis Stevenson)

17. _____: a banker provided by nature (French proverb)

18. _____: the only sure bait when you angle for praise (G. K. Chesterton)

19. _____: something that lengthens your mileage, diminishes your gas, and strengthens your vocabulary (Oliver Herford)

20. _____: the poor man's bread (Thales)

21. _____: a person whom we know well enough to borrow from but not well enough to lend to (Ambrose Bierce)

22. _____: that which is never seen until someone expresses it simply (Kahlil Gibran)

23. _____: the weak man's imitation of strength (Eric Hoffer)

24. _____: history shot on the wing (Gene Fowler)

25. _____: one who uses the cross as a hammer to knock in the heads of sinners (H. L. Mencken)

26. _____: the unbearable repartee (G. K. Chesterton)

27. _____: confession without absolution (G. K. Chesterton)

28. _____: the index of the mind (Seneca)

29. _____: conspiracies against the laity (George Bernard Shaw)

30. _____: the groom at a wedding (Anonymous)

II. You should be ready now to try your hand at writing some especially apt definitions of your own. For each of the words below, look up first the dictionary definition and write it down. Then dream up your *own* definition, making it as vivid and memorable as possible.

1. SADNESS

Dictionary definition: _____

Your definition: _____

2. WAR

   Dictionary definition: _____

   Your definition: _____

3. LAUGHTER

   Dictionary definition: _____

   Your definition: _____

4. EDUCATION

   Dictionary definition: _____

   Your definition: _____

5. FEAR

   Dictionary definition: _____

   Your definition: _____

6. YOUTH

   Dictionary definition: _____

   Your definition: _____

7. JEALOUSY

   Dictionary definition: _____

   Your definition: _____

8. DOCTOR

   Dictionary definition: _____

   Your definition: _____

9. HOMEWORK

   Dictionary definition: _____

   Your definition: _____

10. AUTOMOBILE

   Dictionary definition: _____

   Your definition: _____

9
Spoke Screen

Spoke Screen is a word game that will challenge you and confuse you. The purpose of this game is to complete the spokes of each wheel by inserting words of a certain length that begin and end with the letter in the hub of the wheel.

Definitions are provided to help you complete the first six Spoke Screens. Write each word on a spoke starting at the hub for #1, 2, 3, 4, 5, and 6. (*Clue:* Think about which letters go together naturally: *-ed, -st, tr-, -ch*, etc.)

I. All the words have five letters, beginning and ending with *D*.

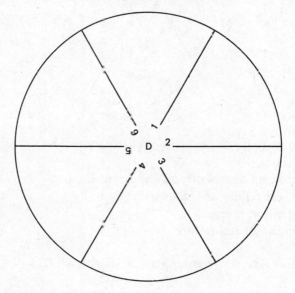

1. stunned; confused
2. ventured; took a chance
3. cut into small cubes (like a potato)
4. stale; out of style
5. shaped like the top half of a head
6. terrible fear; terror

II. All the words have four letters, beginning and ending with *B*.

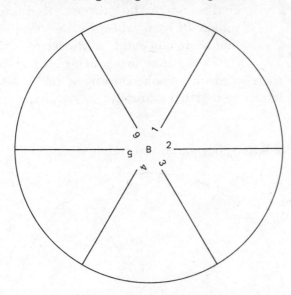

1. sharp, hooked point (e.g., on an arrow); cutting remark
2. simpleton; fool (slang)
3. underground beginning of a plant; incandescent lamp
4. to talk too much, especially about secret things
5. shapeless daub of color; smear
6. an explosive weapon; a total failure

III. All the words have five letters, beginning and ending with *H*.

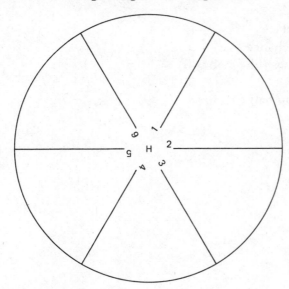

1. intuitive guess; strong feeling
2. severe; stern
3. a pen for rabbits; a cupboard with open shelves
4. an opening in the deck of a ship leading to the hold
5. to fasten with a rope; to thumb a ride
6. a moor; a large tract of uncultivated land with some small bushes and plants

Wide World of Words

IV. All the words have five letters, beginning and ending with *L*.

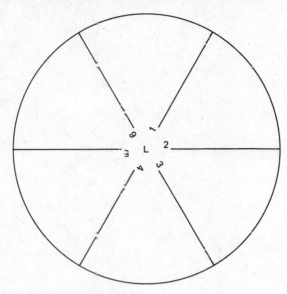

1. extension of coat or jacket collar
2. even; balanced
3. pertaining to a specific place; making many stops
4. a statement that damages a person's reputation
5. an identification tag
6. according to the law

V. All the words have five letters, beginning and ending with *R*.

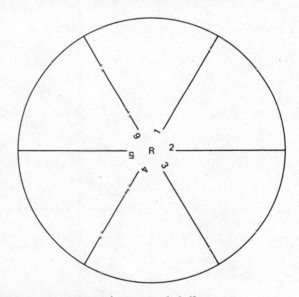

1. a sharp-edged instrument, sometimes used daily
2. rotating part of a machine
3. one who wanders around
4. gossip; talk without a sure source
5. one who controls and governs
6. a natural stream of water larger than a brook or creek

VI. All the words have five letters, beginning and ending with *T*.

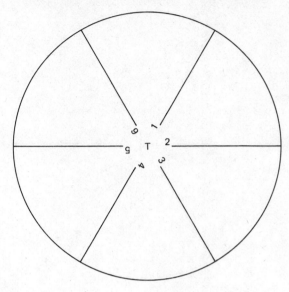

1. ridicule; jeer at
2. to contaminate; to corrupt
3. a distinguishing feature
4. a freshwater fish
5. confidence
6. a secret meeting

VII. Here are a couple of spoke screens on which you can experiment.

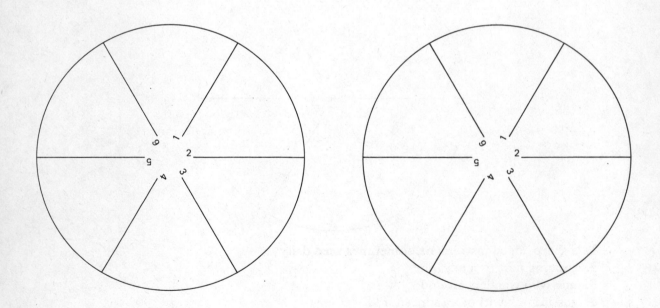

Eleven. Wordplay

1 Casual Crosswords

Practically everyone likes to do crossword puzzles. They're challenging, relaxing, and fun. If you have never before tried to do one, begin now with these "Casual Crosswords." They are shorter and easier than most regular puzzles.

To begin, look at the first one below. Take a quick look at the definitions. Choose one that you know. #4 Down, for example—an "airtight metal container." A *can*, probably. Write the letters in the squares, starting with the #4 square. Now use these letters as aids in finding other words. #7 Across is "impoverished; deprived of necessities." You need a five-letter word beginning with "n." These clues should help you to think of *needy*. Continue, following the same procedure.

I.

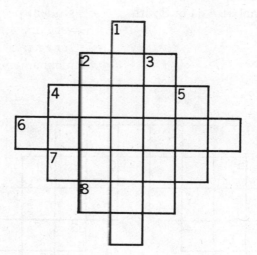

ACROSS

2. existed
4. proofreading mark
6. pesters; annoys
7. impoverished; deprived of necessities
8. enclosure for pigs

DOWN

1. objects fired at; goals
2. walks through water
3. shabby in appearance
4. airtight metal container
5. attempt; strive

II.

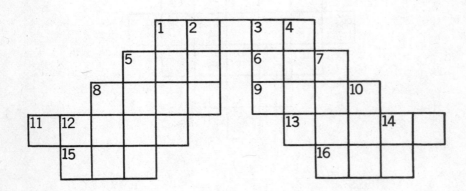

ACROSS

1. daily or weekly publication containing news
9. fastened tightly; tied up
10. short-legged mammal of Asia or South America
11. make free; relieve

DOWN

2. plural ending
3. not dry
4. mark left by a wound
5. student
6. very dry
7. for each
8. nickname for Edward

III.

ACROSS

1. smooth, lustrous gem
5. moved rapidly
6. be ill
8. difficult; not soft
9. overfill; satiate
11. bell with a musical sound
13. group of soldiers
15. small snake
16. very long period of time

DOWN

1. peel; cut down
2. the last point or part of a thing
3. tatter
4. a swinging movement or rhythm
5. inclined roadway or passage
7. attract; entice
8. possessive form of "he"
10. excessively; also
12. exclamation showing amusement
14. atop

IV.

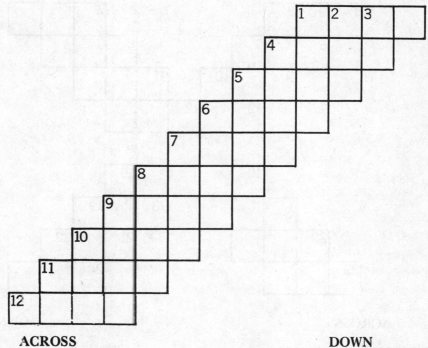

ACROSS

1. good, better, _____
4. single race
5. wild pig
6. to speak indistinctly
7. found at entrance to a room
8. young horse
9. not barefoot
10. slender
11. poetic word for ocean
12. female student in a school for males and females

DOWN

1. mammal with shaggy coat; sometimes dances
2. auditory organ
3. abbreviation for street
4. sixty minutes
5. stain, especially of ink
6. exchanged for money
7. disaster; terrible fate
8. bit of wood
9. vehicle for traveling over snow
10. observe; notice
11. perform; act

V.

ACROSS

1. floor pad
4. wicked; disagreeable
6. sticky substance
8. order; make an offer
9. one who overeats (slang)
11. sink; droop
12. bestow; to agree to
14. trouble; fuss
15. prevent; ward off
17. exist
18. very long time
20. minute insect
21. fenced enclosure
23. termination
24. child's plaything

DOWN

2. near; by
3. knock; rap softly
4. large
5. public notice (abbrev.)
7. equipment
8. club used to hit a ball
10. solemn; serious
11. make a noise while sleeping
13. a sweetened drink made from water and fruit juice
15. aesthetic work
16. uppermost part of something
17. connective
19. device for catching fish
20. article
22. negative answer

Wide World of Words

2
Add-a-Letter

Because all words in English are composed of the 26 letters of the alphabet, in different combinations, all resemble each other a little. Some resemble each other a great deal. Consider the word *all*. Place a *b* in front of it, and you have _____ , a child's toy. Place an *m* in front of it, and you have _____ , a shaded walk.

I. In this exercise you are given a central word and asked to create new words by adding *one* letter each time at the beginning of the word. The number of new words you should be able to create is indicated by the number of incomplete words that follow the central word. (Since *qu* always appears as a unit, in this exercise *qu* counts as one letter.)

1. AID

    a. __aid   *c.* __aid

    b. __aid   *d.* __aid

          e. __aid

2. ODE

    a. __ode   *d.* __ode

    b. __ode   *e.* __ode

    c. __ode   *f.* __ode

3. ONE

    a. __one   *e.* __one

    b. __one   *f.* __one

    c. __one   *g.* __one

    d. __one   *h.* __one

          i. __one

4. AIL

    a. __ail   *g.* __ail

    b. __ail   *h.* __ail

    c. __ail   *i.* __ail

    d. __ail   *j.* __ail

    e. __ail   *k.* __ail

    f. __ail   *l.* __ail

5. ILL

    a. __ill   *g.* __ill

    b. __ill   *h.* __ill

    c. __ill   *i.* __ill

    d. __ill   *j.* __ill

    e. __ill   *k.* __ill

    f. __ill   *l.* __ill

          m. __ill

II. Here's a twist on the add-a-letter game. In each cluster below, the first word and its definition are given. The second word's definition is given, but you must find the word by adding a letter at the end of the word. Find the third word by adding still another letter at the beginning of the word.

1. arc (something curved)

   arc__ (usually curved part of a structure over an opening)

   __arc__ (a regular even step used by soldiers)

2. ran (moved rapidly)

   ran__ (to speak violently and loudly)

   __ran__ (to bestow)

3. tin (metallic element)

   tin__ (shade of color)

   __tin__ (fixed amount of work to be performed)

III. Now it's time for a more sophisticated approach. Again, the first word and its definition are given. To form the remaining words, though, you may have to add a letter at the beginning, in the middle, or at the end. You may feel slightly addled when you have finished this one!

1. at (preposition suggesting direction or location)

   a__t (aesthetic work)

   __a__t (male deer)

   ____a__t (central part)

   ____a__t__ (floor of a fireplace)

2. ad (public notice)

   __ad (wicked; disagreeable)

   __ad__ (ordered)

   __ad____ (emblem; characteristic mark)

   __ad_____ (to pester; also, a small carnivorous animal)

3. id (part of the psyche)

   __id (to make free; to relieve)

   __id__ (to sit on and control)

   ____id__ (woman about to be married)

   ____id____ (structure spanning a river)

3
Change-about

This word game calls for a fast eye and a quick mind. It is based on the manipulation of letters.

Step I. Change the first word into the last word by changing one letter at a time. Do not change the *order* of the letters.

Example: bait to tell (4 steps)
Answer: bait-bail-tail-tall-tell

Now try these.

1. *come* to *dirk*   (4 steps) _____
2. *rage* to *both*   (4 steps) _____
3. *bead* to *loon*   (4 steps) _____
4. *kiss* to *mart*   (4 steps) _____
5. *mare* to *colt*   (4 steps) _____
6. *pond* to *lake*   (4 steps) _____
7. *lion* to *hare*   (6 steps) _____
8. *girl* to *wife*   (4 steps) _____
9. *sand* to *bore*   (4 steps) _____
10. *cash* to *boat*   (4 steps) _____

Step II. Change one letter in the first word to make the second word, one in the second word to make the third, etc. Note the definitions.

1. *a.* DREAM
   b. _____ terror; great fear
   c. _____ to walk on or over
   d. _____ staple of life
   e. _____ to shatter; to split
   f. _____ dreary; cheerless

2. *a.* STILE
   b. _____ long fur scarf worn around the shoulders
   c. _____ trite; no longer fresh
   d. _____ to climb
   e. _____ to burn with hot liquid or steam
   f. _____ to chide; to reprimand

3. *a.* TRAIT

    b. _____ engine plus cars

    c. _____ part of body that controls emotion and thought

    d. _____ to interweave; to plait

    e. _____ trademark identifying a product

    f. _____ pleasant; soothing; nonirritating

4. *a.* PROBE

    b. _____ to establish the truth of

    c. _____ small woods

    d. _____ to feel one's way; to search uncertainly

    e. _____ small round fruit of a vine

    f. _____ to let fall in loose folds

5. *a.* SWING

    b. _____ a loose strap or rope for supporting something

    c. _____ to sneak; to move furtively

    d. _____ to look with half-shut winking eyes

    e. _____ unable to see

    f. _____ light-colored, as of hair and furniture

4

Pyramid Play

Building pyramids was challenging, even to the ancient Egyptians. Building word pyramids can be challenging, too.

I. Build a pyramid of words, using the seven clues given below. All the words needed to complete this pyramid begin and end with the letter "s." In fact, all are plurals. The number of blanks corresponds to the number of letters in the word.

$$\_\ \_\ \_\ \_\ \_$$

$$\_\ \_\ \_\ \_\ \_\ \_$$

$$\_\ \_\ \_\ \_\ \_\ \_\ \_$$

$$\_\ \_\ \_\ \_\ \_\ \_\ \_\ \_$$

$$\_\ \_\ \_\ \_\ \_\ \_\ \_\ \_\ \_$$

$$\_\ \_\ \_\ \_\ \_\ \_\ \_\ \_\ \_\ \_$$

1st line: long, flat runners useful for traveling over snow
2nd line: marks left by wounds or injuries
3rd line: pointed structures often forming the tops of churches
4th line: short, violent windstorms
5th line: enlisted men in the army
6th line: bony structures of vertebrates
7th line: sellers of paper, pens, etc.

II. Now try this one. All words begin and end with "d." All are in the past tense.

$$\_\ \_\ \_\ \_\ \_$$

$$\_\ \_\ \_\ \_\ \_\ \_$$

$$\_\ \_\ \_\ \_\ \_\ \_\ \_$$

$$\_\ \_\ \_\ \_\ \_\ \_\ \_\ \_$$

$$\_\ \_\ \_\ \_\ \_\ \_\ \_\ \_\ \_$$

$$\_\ \_\ \_\ \_\ \_\ \_\ \_\ \_\ \_\ \_$$

1st line: made a new color
2nd line: ate
3rd line: selected a TV channel; placed a telephone call
4th line: separated into parts
5th line: gave letters orally to a stenographer
6th line: melted; became liquid
7th line: took apart

III. This one uses present participles, verb forms ending in "ing." All of the words begin and end with "g."

———————

———————

————————

—————————

——————————

———————————

      1st line: moving along; proceeding
      2nd line: donating
      3rd line: biting; chewing
      4th line: taking a quick look
      5th line: accumulating; collecting
      6th line: sparkling brilliantly

IV. On this pyramid, all words begin and end with "n."

———

————

—————

——————

———————

————————

      1st line: woman who has taken religious vows
      2nd line: name of a person, place, or thing
      3rd line: synthetic material
      4th line: country
      5th line: wooden pin used in an old game
      6th line: memo; comment; jotting

V. On this one, all words begin and end with "p."

            — — — —
           — — — — —
         — — — — —
       — — — — — —
      — — — — — — —
    — — — — — — — —
   — — — — — — — — —
  — — — — — — — — —

1st line: soft food
2nd line: soft part of fruit; cheap magazine
3rd line: chubby; well-rounded
4th line: adjective used to describe a light, open truck
5th line: strong-scented, edible plant
6th line: business place where one may borrow money
            after leaving personal property as security
7th line: adjective used to describe a landing made by
            armed people jumping out of an airplane
8th line: style of handwriting

5
From One, Many!

Here's a word game that you can play anytime, anywhere. You will need only pencil and paper. Choose a fairly simple word, like *climate*. Write this word at the top of your sheet of paper. Now make as many words as possible from the original word, following these rules:

1. Use only the letters in the original word. Letters may be omitted, but they may not be added.
2. Use each letter only as often as it appears in the original word.
3. Proper nouns, plurals, and past tenses that end in *-ed* may not be used. (*Added* may not be used, but *seen* is permissible.)
4. Arrange the words you make up in groups beginning with the same letter.
5. If two or more players are playing the game, anyone who questions the existence of a word given by another player may challenge it and consult the dictionary.

Sample word: CLIMATE

ate	clam	eat	item	lime	mat	tea
aim	clime	éclat	ice	lam	mate	tam
ace	cleat	elm		lame	male	tame
ale	cat	emit		late	mail	team
ail	cam			lace	mace	teal
alm	came			lice	mice	tale
act	calm			lima	meat	tail
				lit	mite	tie
				lea	melt	time
				let	mile	tile
				lie	malt	

Some helpful hints:

1. Remember that some consonants pair off as initial sounds, e.g., "cl." This leads to "clam," "clime," and "cleat."
2. Remember that some consonants pair off as final sounds, e.g., "lm." This leads to "calm," "alm," and "elm."
3. Try rhymes. "Ace" may lead you to "mace" and "lace."

Now try this same procedure on other words.
Later try these variations:

1. How many four-letter words can you create from *archipelago* (a group of islands)? (Aim for 50 words.)

----

2. How many words beginning with a vowel (a, e, i, o, u) can you create from *parsonage?* (Aim for 15 words.)

----

3. How many nouns (name-words) can you create from *spectacles?* (Aim for 50 words.)

----

4. How many words of two or more letters can you create from *condiment* (seasoning for food)? (Aim for *at least* 75 words!)

6
Acrostic Crossfire

An acrostic, in its simplest form, is a name the letters of which form the first letters of successive lines of verse or prose. For example:

M ary is a clever girl,
A s good as she is bright;
R abid fans applaud for her
Y odeling in the night.

There are all sorts of ways of playing acrostics.

I. Let's begin by testing your aptitude for acrostics with a simple exercise. Take two proper names that go together and that have the same number of letters: LAKE ERIE. Write them vertically, then form words that begin with the letters in the first column and end with the letters in the second column.

Example: L eisur E (leisure)
A bho R (abhor)
K hak I (khaki)
E stimat E (estimate)

Here are some for you to try. (All words, except proper names, are acceptable.)

1. U _ _ _ _ _ _ _ _ _ _ _ _ _ _ _ S
N _ _ _ _ _ _ _ _ _ _ _ _ _ _ _ T
I _ _ _ _ _ _ _ _ _ _ _ _ _ _ _ A
T _ _ _ _ _ _ _ _ _ _ _ _ _ _ _ T
E _ _ _ _ _ _ _ _ _ _ _ _ _ _ _ E
D _ _ _ _ _ _ _ _ _ _ _ _ _ _ _ S

2. R _ _ _ _ _ _ _ _ _ _ _ _ _ _ _ S
E _ _ _ _ _ _ _ _ _ _ _ _ _ _ _ E
D _ _ _ _ _ _ _ _ _ _ _ _ _ _ _ A

3. N _ _ _ _ _ _ _ _ _ _ _ _ _ _ _ T
A _ _ _ _ _ _ _ _ _ _ _ _ _ _ _ E
S _ _ _ _ _ _ _ _ _ _ _ _ _ _ _ N
H _ _ _ _ _ _ _ _ _ _ _ _ _ _ _ N
V _ _ _ _ _ _ _ _ _ _ _ _ _ _ _ E
I _ _ _ _ _ _ _ _ _ _ _ _ _ _ _ S
L _ _ _ _ _ _ _ _ _ _ _ _ _ _ _ S
L _ _ _ _ _ _ _ _ _ _ _ _ _ _ _ E
E _ _ _ _ _ _ _ _ _ _ _ _ _ _ _ E

4. S _ _ _ _ _ _ _ _ _ _ _ _ _ _ _ C
A _ _ _ _ _ _ _ _ _ _ _ _ _ _ _ A
C _ _ _ _ _ _ _ _ _ _ _ _ _ _ _ L
R _ _ _ _ _ _ _ _ _ _ _ _ _ _ _ I
A _ _ _ _ _ _ _ _ _ _ _ _ _ _ _ F
M _ _ _ _ _ _ _ _ _ _ _ _ _ _ _ O
E _ _ _ _ _ _ _ _ _ _ _ _ _ _ _ R
N _ _ _ _ _ _ _ _ _ _ _ _ _ _ _ N
T _ _ _ _ _ _ _ _ _ _ _ _ _ _ _ I
O _ _ _ _ _ _ _ _ _ _ _ _ _ _ _ A

5. A - - - - - - - - - - - - - - G   6. T - - - - - - - - - - - - - - K

    T - - - - - - - - - - - - - E   O - - - - - - - - - - - - - - A

    L - - - - - - - - - - - - - O   P - - - - - - - - - - - - - - N

    A - - - - - - - - - - - - - R   E - - - - - - - - - - - - - - S

    N - - - - - - - - - - - - - G   K - - - - - - - - - - - - - - A

    T - - - - - - - - - - - - - I   A - - - - - - - - - - - - - - S

    A - - - - - - - - - - - - - A

II. This time take a first name and write a sentence, each word beginning with a letter of the name.

Examples: J ump   D on't

                   A long,   A ntagonize

                   C owardly   V oters

                   K angaroo!   I n

                                  D elaware.

Try these:

1. K - - - - - - - - - - - - - - - - -   2. R - - - - - - - - - - - - - - - - -

    A - - - - - - - - - - - - - - - - -   I - - - - - - - - - - - - - - - - -

    R - - - - - - - - - - - - - - - - -   C - - - - - - - - - - - - - - - - -

    E - - - - - - - - - - - - - - - - -   H - - - - - - - - - - - - - - - - -

    N - - - - - - - - - - - - - - - - -   A - - - - - - - - - - - - - - - - -

                                              R - - - - - - - - - - - - - - - - -

                                              D - - - - - - - - - - - - - - - - -

3. M - - - - - - - - - - - - - - - - -   4. M - - - - - - - - - - - - - - - - -

    I - - - - - - - - - - - - - - - - -   A - - - - - - - - - - - - - - - - -

    C - - - - - - - - - - - - - - - - -   R - - - - - - - - - - - - - - - - -

    H - - - - - - - - - - - - - - - - -   I - - - - - - - - - - - - - - - - -

    A - - - - - - - - - - - - - - - - -   A - - - - - - - - - - - - - - - - -

    E - - - - - - - - - - - - - - - - -

    L - - - - - - - - - - - - - - - - -

Try one with your own name and another with the name of a friend.

------------------------   ------------------------
------------------------   ------------------------
------------------------   ------------------------
------------------------   ------------------------
------------------------   ------------------------
------------------------   ------------------------

III. As a final test for an aptitude for acrostics, write a short acrostic poem like the one in the first paragraph of this lesson. Choose your own name (or any other name you like), and create an acrostic poem.

7

Circle Circus

Most circuses have three rings of activity for spectators. So this is something different—a five-ring circus—perfect for some acrobatics with words!

I. Moving clockwise (left to right) on the circle below, try to find at least 8 animal-related words and 10 other words without skipping any boxes. For example, starting at the top of the circle, the first letter is *W*, the second *O*, the third *L*, and the fourth *F*; together they form the word *WOLF*.

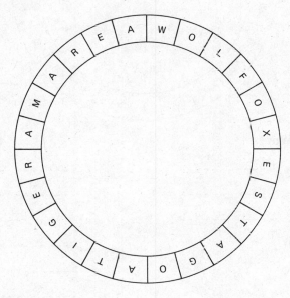

Animal Words			Other Words	
-----------	-----------		-----------	-----------
-----------	-----------		-----------	-----------
-----------	-----------		-----------	-----------
-----------	-----------		-----------	-----------
			-----------	-----------

II. This time find 6 color words and 12 other words.

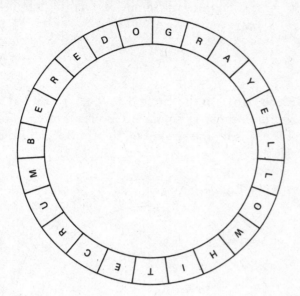

<table>
<tr><td style="text-align:center">Color Words</td><td style="text-align:center">Other Words</td></tr>
</table>

Color Words			Other Words	
- - - - - - - - - - -	- - - - - - - - - - -		- - - - - - - - - -	- - - - - - - - - - -
- - - - - - - - - - -	- - - - - - - - - - -		- - - - - - - - - -	- - - - - - - - - - -
- - - - - - - - - - -	- - - - - - - - - - -		- - - - - - - - - -	- - - - - - - - - - -
			- - - - - - - - - -	- - - - - - - - - - -
			- - - - - - - - - -	- - - - - - - - - - -
			- - - - - - - - - -	- - - - - - - - - - -

III. In this ring, find 6 flower words and 10 other words.

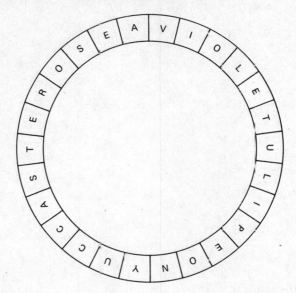

Flower Words

---------- ----------

---------- ----------

---------- ----------

Other Words

---------- ----------

---------- ----------

---------- ----------

---------- ----------

---------- ----------

IV. In this ring, find 8 words that name parts of the body and 8 other words:

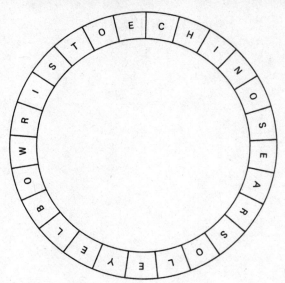

<table>
<tr><th colspan="2">Body Words</th><th colspan="2">Other Words</th></tr>
<tr><td>-----------</td><td>-----------</td><td>-----------</td><td>-----------</td></tr>
<tr><td>-----------</td><td>-----------</td><td>-----------</td><td>-----------</td></tr>
<tr><td>-----------</td><td>-----------</td><td>-----------</td><td>-----------</td></tr>
<tr><td>-----------</td><td>-----------</td><td>-----------</td><td>-----------</td></tr>
</table>

V. This time find words that name 8 objects that might be found around the house, and then find 8 other words:

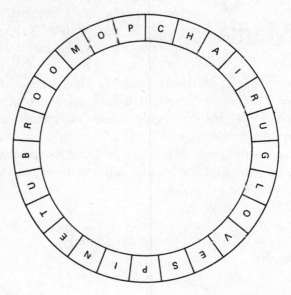

House Words		Other Words	
- - - - - - - - - -	- - - - - - - - - -	- - - - - - - - - -	- - - - - - - - - -
- - - - - - - - - -	- - - - - - - - - -	- - - - - - - - - -	- - - - - - - - - -
- - - - - - - - - -	- - - - - - - - - -	- - - - - - - - - -	- - - - - - - - - -
- - - - - - - - - -	- - - - - - - - - -	- - - - - - - - - -	- - - - - - - - - -

Now, still using circle V, go into reverse (counterclockwise: right to left) and find 8 more words:

In Reverse

- - - - - - - - - -	- - - - - - - - - -
- - - - - - - - - -	- - - - - - - - - -
- - - - - - - - - -	- - - - - - - - - -
- - - - - - - - - -	- - - - - - - - - -

8

Monogram Mania

A monogram is a combination of the two or three initials of someone's name. President Harry S. Truman, for example, was frequently known as simply HST; and President John F. Kennedy became JFK. Finding appropriate phrases to fit the monogram can be an amusing and spirited game.

Abraham Lincoln's monogram, of course, was AL. Since he worked with tree logs, he could be called an "able logger." Since he participated in legal debates, he could also be called an "astute lawyer." And since he is one of the great names and memories in this country's history, he could also be called an "American Legend."

Take part in the game, Monogram Mania, by creating sharp or amusing phrases to fit the monograms of these people. (The first five include definitions to help you get started.)

1. George Washington
   (led the Colonial forces in the American Revolution)
   G _____ (outstanding)   W _____ (one engaged in battle)

2. Thomas Jefferson
   (lawyer; drew up the Declaration of Independence)
   T _____ (contemplative; given to reason)   J _____ (person skilled in the law)

3. Elizabeth Taylor
   (actress)
   E _____ (tasteful and expensive)   T _____ (another word for actor or actress)

4. Daniel Boone
   (explored and settled Kentucky; pioneer)
   D _____ (territory)   B _____ (constructor)

5. Groucho Marx
   (famous comedian)
   G _____ (smiling)   M _____ (nonconformist)

6. Lucille Ball
   (famous comedian)
   L _____   B _____

7. Joe Louis
   (heavyweight boxing champion, 1937–49)
   J _____   L _____

8. Barbra Streisand
   (popular singer)
   B _____   S _____

9. Dwight Eisenhower
   (U.S. President, and general in World War II)
   D _____   E _____

10. Humphrey Bogart
    (tough-guy actor)
    H _____   B _____

11. Ernest Hemingway
(novelist who wrote about wars
and bullfights)

E _ _ _ _ _ _ _ _ _ _ _ _ _ _ _   H _ _ _ _ _ _ _ _ _ _ _ _ _ _ _

12. Marlon Brando
(actor)

M _ _ _ _ _ _ _ _ _ _ _ _ _ _ _   B _ _ _ _ _ _ _ _ _ _ _ _ _ _ _

13. Susan B. Anthony
(early leader of woman suffrage)

S _ _ _ _ _ _ _ _ _ _ _ _ _ _ _   A _ _ _ _ _ _ _ _ _ _ _ _ _ _ _

14. Napoleon Bonaparte
(powerful French general and
emperor)

N _ _ _ _ _ _ _ _ _ _ _ _ _ _ _   B _ _ _ _ _ _ _ _ _ _ _ _ _ _ _

15. Albert Einstein
(physicist who developed the
theory of relativity)

A _ _ _ _ _ _ _ _ _ _ _ _ _ _ _   E _ _ _ _ _ _ _ _ _ _ _ _ _ _ _

Just for fun, fill in names of your own choosing (not necessarily those of celebrities) on lines 16 through 20. Then develop phrases that match their monograms.

16. _   _ _ _ _ _ _ _ _ _ _ _ _ _ _   _ _ _ _ _ _ _ _ _ _ _ _ _ _

17. _   _ _ _ _ _ _ _ _ _ _ _ _ _ _   _ _ _ _ _ _ _ _ _ _ _ _ _ _

18. _   _ _ _ _ _ _ _ _ _ _ _ _ _ _   _ _ _ _ _ _ _ _ _ _ _ _ _ _

19. _   _ _ _ _ _ _ _ _ _ _ _ _ _ _   _ _ _ _ _ _ _ _ _ _ _ _ _ _

20. _   _ _ _ _ _ _ _ _ _ _ _ _ _ _   _ _ _ _ _ _ _ _ _ _ _ _ _ _

9

Harebrained Homonyms

Homonyms are words that sound alike but are different in spelling and in meaning. Manipulating them can result in your gaining *sense* (but not necessarily *cents*)!

I. Each of the following couplets contains clues to a pair of homonyms. For example, if someone recites

> He sells all his wares,
> But never upstairs.

you will instantly deduce that he is talking about a *cellar seller*. Wouldn't you?

Try to find the pair of homonyms appropriate for each of the following bits of verse:

1. Bruno and Smoky at times he is called.
   Strip off his hair, and he's more than just bald.

   ----

2. The children love Bambi, all parents agree,
   But to buy one, remember, entails a large fee.

   ----

3. Though for long unemployed, he is still very proud:
   He's a movie star cheered and adored by the crowd.

   ----

4. The hen tumbled into a basin of muck;
   The ill-smelling chicken's sure down on her luck.

   ----

5. At thirteen years he became a mole,
   Digging all day for lumps of coal.

The rest of these paired homonyms operate without benefit of verse. Let the definition guide you to the answer.

6. Someone who lives in a boardinghouse on the boundary line between the United

   States and Mexico might be called a ------------------------------ .

7. A thoroughbred with a sore throat is probably a ------------------------------ .

8. Unfriendly lodgings for a young, not-very-confident traveller constitute a ----------

   ------------------------------ .

9. The borrowing of money, just one time, may be described as a ------------------

   ------------------------------ .

10. A wooden bucket that has been bleached by the sun is a ------------------------.

11. A cute group of connected rooms is a ------------------------------ .

12. A correct ceremonial act is a ---------------------------------- .

13. A miserly or spiteful manner is a ---------------------------------- .

II. Use the following definitions to help you create catchy titles:

1. The story of an appendage, or

   A ----------------- of a ----------------

2. A dock without equal, or

   A ---------------- Without ----------------

3. To pretend to swoon, or

   To ---------------- a ----------------

4. A tree on a sandy coast, or

   A ---------------- on a ----------------

5. Eight hours of darkness for a medieval gentleman-soldier, or

   A ----------------'s ----------------

III. Complete the following sentences by inserting the correct pair of homonyms:

1. He --------------- just after he had his hair -------------- red, but apparently the two events were not related.

2. " --------------- , ---------------- , sir," -------------- said to the Captain, as -------------- winked one -------------- .

3. "You must -------------- yourself not to -------------- ," said the parson to the steely-eyed pickpocket.

4. Father to long-haired son: "Have the barber take off the -------------- part of that -------------- !"

5. One scratching dog to another scratching dog: "Make the -------------- -------------- !"

6. Parent to offspring: "If you are -------------- once more for speeding, -------------- yourself a new banker!"

7. Child to parent at post office: "Look, mommy—a non-------------- --------------man!"

8. Melodramatic: -------------- to a post at the water's edge, he watched with horror as the -------------- came in.

9. Quizzical: If she is a genuine -------------- , why doesn't she -------------- from her ability to foretell the future?

10. Practical: To lose weight, eat meat but -------------- -------------- .

Topical Reference Guide

In this book, word study centers around the topics listed below.

Advertising, 94–96
Animals, 102–129, 138–139, 141–144, 188–190
Aquatic terms, 151–153
Archery, 148–149
Automobiles, 156–159
Aviation, 169–171
Avocations, 203–204
Bicycles, 160–161
Birds, 112–115
Birthstones, 196–199
Body, parts of the, 208–209
Clothes, 36–40
Colors, 121, 191–193
Computers, 181
Criminals, 17–18
Criminology, 1–25
Cycles, 160–162
Detection, crime, 1–25
Education, 48–51
Evidence, legal, 18
Fashion, 36–40
Fencing, 149
Films, 83–85

Fingerprints, 4–6
Fish, 109
Flowers, 200–202
Food, 41–43
Gems, 196–199
Geographical terms, 52–54
Horses 121–122, 138–139, 141–144
Houses and other residences, 44–47
 parts of a house, 26
Humor, 57–77
Ice skating, 145–146
Identification, police methods of, 1–3
Insects, 116–118
Jewels, 196–199
Laughter, 57–59
Mass media, 78–101
Materials (textiles, etc.), 37
Metals, 194–195
Monsters, 174–176
Moon, the, 179
Motion pictures, 83–85

Motorcycles, 161–162
Moulages, 7
Newspapers, 86–87
Photography, 91–93
Policemen and police work, 17–19
Politics, 97–99
Racing, 137–140
Racquet games, 134–136
Radio, 88–90
Railroads, 166–168
Rogues' gallery, 20
Roller derby, 163–164
Schools, 48–51
Skiing, 145
Space travel, 177–180
Sports, 130–155
Television, 81–82
Tools, 28
Travel, 52–54, 156–173
Vocations, 203–204
Water sports, 151–153
Wheels, 163–165
Winter sports, 145–147
Zoos, 106–108

Index

Abbreviations, 157
Acronyms, 152, 178–179
Acrostics, 250–252
Analogies, 119, 149
Antonyms, 34, 222–224
Appearance, of words, 72–74
Boners, 70
Codes, 215–216
Comic strips, 75–77
Couplets, 66, 155, 260
Crossword puzzles, 237–240
Deduction, 11
Definitions, memorable, 230–231
Epithets, 119–120
Gobbledegook, 64–65
Homonyms, 260–261
Hyperbole, 109
Irish bulls, 69
Limericks, 67
Monograms, 258–259
Names
 first, 210–211
 place-, 211–212
 proper, 200–201
Namesakes, 11–13, 200–201
Proverbs, 36, 40, 43, 61, 63
Puns, 60–62

Quatrains, 66–67
Riddles, 60–62
Slips, in language, 69–71
Sounds, of words, 72–74, 222
Spoonerisms, 70–71
Word elements
 aer, 169
 animus, 4
 anti, 169
 auto, 156, 169
 bi, 160
 black, 192
 blue, 192
 color, 191
 dis, 223
 down, 223
 egg, 42–43
 grand, 205
 green, 191
 high, 223
 horse, 143–144
 il, 223
 in, 223
 ir, 223
 land, 206
 line, 205

 low, 223
 lower, 223
 magni, 4
 mal, 106, 107
 micro, 4
 mini, 11, 13
 naut, 169
 non, 223
 omni, 102, 104
 out, 205
 over, 223
 phono, 4
 red, 191
 scope, 4
 sign, 206
 stock, 205
 sub, 14
 super, 169
 time, 206
 tri, 160
 un, 223
 under, 223
 uni, 160
 up, 223
 upper, 223
 white, 192